The Old Roads of

DERBYSHIRE

The Old Roads of Derbyshire

WALKING INTO HISTORY: THE PORTWAY AND BEYOND

Stephen Bailey

Matador
9 Priory Business Park,
Wistow Road, Kibworth Beauchamp,
Leicestershire, LE8 0RX
Tel: 0116 279 2299
Email: books@troubador.co.uk
Web: www.troubador.co.uk/matador
Twitter: @matadorbooks

ISBN 978 1789018 431

British Library Cataloguing in Publication Data.
A catalogue record for this book is available from the British Library.

Printed and bound by CPI Group (UK) Ltd, Croydon, CR0 4YY
Typeset in 11pt Adobe Caslon Pro by Troubador Publishing Ltd, Leicester, UK

Matador is an imprint of Troubador Publishing Ltd

Dedicated to all those who work to preserve and maintain the public footpaths and bridleways of England.

Contents

Preface

My previous book, *The Derbyshire Portway: Pilgrimage to the Past*, attempted to trace the route of this ancient trackway across Derbyshire, from the Nottinghamshire border near Stapleford to Mam Tor in the north. Since then the Portway has been featured in several television programmes and has inspired a series of paintings by the Derbyshire artist Lindsey Hambleton. One of these is reproduced on the back cover of the current book.

Subsequently, however, I have become aware of some limitations in the original book, not least the start and end points, and so I have tried to extend the route southeastwards by examining the area between the Hemlock Stone and Sneinton in Nottingham, and at the northern end from Mam Tor into the Woodlands Valley. Additionally, more research has been published, such as details of the Wirksworth team's excavations of the Portway between Bakewell and Wirksworth. Students in my WEA classes have shared useful local knowledge, and listeners to my talks in village halls around the county have made many helpful comments. I have also increasingly recognised the importance of features such as guide stoops, wayside crosses, river crossings and road names in unravelling the pattern of the past.

Consequently, the present book is both an extension of my previous study and an expansion of the subject beyond the history of the one road. I am interested in tracing not only the ancient routes through the landscape but also suggesting who could have been using them: it is the story of travellers as well as travel. There are few documentary sources available before the late seventeenth century to tell us the names of Derbyshire wayfarers, but it is reasonable to assume, for instance, that this county, in common with other English regions, had its Christian pilgrims in the Middle Ages.

While we can never hope to establish definitively the road system of, say, medieval England, which must have been constantly changing due to economic, political, climatic and other pressures, we can fairly safely assume that certain routes have been in use for many hundreds of years. *The Old Roads of Derbyshire* identifies some of these routes and puts them into the wider context of the development of the county's roads from prehistoric times until the end of the nineteenth century. Overall, the aim is to provide an overview of travel over the centuries rather than a detailed description of changes to particular routes.

Nonetheless, the longest chapter – Chapter 8 – provides a complete walking guide to the entire presumed route of the Portway from Nottingham into the Dark Peak, a route which illustrates many of the issues raised in earlier chapters. Most walkers have some interest in history, and many historians enjoy walking, so I hope that both groups will find the book rewarding. Many of the ideas put forward here are exploratory, and readers might disagree with some of them. I am always glad to hear from anyone with a view on the subject, or a suggestion or criticism to offer.

Acknowledgements

I would like to thank all the students who contributed their knowledge and enthusiasm to my classes with the Workers Educational Association (WEA), the friends who have walked parts of these routes with me, and above all my wife Rene (also my hard worked copy-editor) and daughter Sophie, who have had to listen to me talking about roads for all these years!

Stephen Bailey
stephen.bailey@w3z.co.uk

Introduction

RESEARCHING ROADS

As a general rule, both archaeologists and historians have tended to avoid the topic of roads. Excavations generally focus on more immediately rewarding subjects such as burials or settlements, while the documentary trail is often sparse. As will be shown later, roads are difficult to date with any precision, and consequently historians discuss sites such as Dale Abbey without any mention of how people travelled to and from such an important institution.

An impression has developed that Britain, both before and after Roman times, was a trackless island, where most people stayed at home, and that even in the later Middle Ages most roads were virtually impassable due to extreme neglect, when only the bravest made significant journeys. Yet more recent studies[1] have begun to question this simplistic view, which is also challenged in this book.

Today most people have a mental map of the modern road network of their region. We know, for example, that the main route north from Derby, the A6, runs up the valley of the River Derwent, and so we assume that this has always been the case. But if we study the roads of three hundred years ago, that pre-turnpike network looks very different: the A6 route effectively disappears. Moreover, travellers in early eighteenth-century Derbyshire could have no mental map, since no viable road map of the county had ever been surveyed.

Another difficulty in this field of research is our concept of 'road' as a hard, engineered surface occupying a defined, bounded space. It seems likely that in the pre-enclosure landscape travellers used 'routes', which might shift from side to side as one section became muddy and impassable: such routes might in fact be hundreds of yards wide. There is also a tendency to label some routes as 'drove roads', 'coffin paths' or 'saltways', as if these were their only uses, whereas the kinds of goods carried or animals driven along these roads must have been very varied.

And roads can fade away. We know that there were roads linking important centres in Derbyshire, such as the Roman 'Ryknild Street' (see below) between Derby and Chesterfield. Today, part of this route, near Clay Cross, is a busy modern road (the A61). Yet further south, for example near Pentrich, there is no visible trace of the line of the road at all. If a properly engineered road can disappear, then older prehistoric routes, which presumably were never engineered, can totally fade from

The pre-turnpike road from Cromford to Lea in Bow Wood.

view. Nonetheless, topography can be a useful guide, and stretches of the A61 south of Chesterfield clearly demonstrate its origins as a ridgeway, very probably of pre-Roman date. The assumption that the Roman invaders came to an untamed land seems widespread, but there is increasing recognition that not all Roman roads followed virgin routes, and that many used older trajectories (see Chapter 2).

DATING

Many old roads survive as footpaths or bridle paths, thanks to England's well-marked network of rights of way, and walking these may yield clues to their history. For instance, if a path passes through a set of old stone gateposts, it suggests that this was once used by wheeled vehicles such as carts. Comparing footpath networks on modern maps with paths on Ordnance Survey maps from the nineteenth century shows that surprisingly little has changed. Yet, vital though it is, field work can be misleading. It is commonly asserted that a certain track 'feels' ancient, but this is remarkably difficult to prove. Mossy stone walls, for example, may be only a couple of hundred years old, dating back to an early nineteenth-century enclosure road.

However, the dating of roads can be attempted by various methods. An obvious one is excavation: if Roman foundations are revealed, or datable objects such as coins are found, then this road was in use at that period. Another possibility is to assume that certain sites required convenient access. The Roman road that ran northwest from Brassington to Buxton passed close by a number of ancient sites, including Arbor Low and Minninglow, so that it seems reasonable to suppose that this route pre-dates the Roman occupation and may be over four thousand years old. Similarly, documentary evidence can show that a road was in existence at a certain date: monastic charters sometimes name roads which acted as boundaries to their estates (see

Appendix 5), or old roads were used to mark parish boundaries when these were first established, possibly pre-Conquest. Of course, all these methods simply mean that the road was in use at that time; it may be much older.

MYSTICAL ROADS?

The topic of old roads seems to exert an almost spiritual fascination for some. It may be the romantic notion that a certain route has been trodden for thousands of years, or perhaps it is a relic from the days of pilgrimage when journeys were seen as holy, but whatever the reason, this can lead to some bizarre notions. The most famous example is Alfred Watkins' book *The Old Straight Track*, first published in 1925 and still in print, which claims that ancient Britain was covered in a network of straight paths which linked up key points such as barrows or stone circles. This theory of 'ley lines' has seduced thousands into ruling pencil lines all over Ordnance Survey maps, while ignoring the basic drawback of such an imaginary network: that a straight line is not the easiest route to travel along, especially in hill country.

Later writers who have exploited this seam include Robert Macfarlane (*The Old Ways*, 2012) and Graham Robb (*The Ancient Paths*, 2013). Although anything which gets people outdoors and wandering round the countryside is presumably a good thing, students of history should beware of this tendency to evoke a mythical or mystical past or to make assumptions based on little evidence. For example, the name 'Ryknild Street' appears on the OS map in Gothic script, and is frequently used for naming the road between Little Chester near Derby and Chesterfield, but there is no evidence that the Romans actually called it that. In fact, there is little evidence that the Romans gave names to any of their British roads, although this was a well-documented custom in Italy (e.g. The Appian Way, named after a Roman censor).

MAPS

All researchers of roads need to be familiar with maps of their area, which, despite their limitations, are an invaluable tool. But, as is the case with most English counties, there are no road maps of Derbyshire before the mid-eighteenth century, when Peter Burdett completed his survey of the county in1767.[2] Earlier maps may survive for individual estates or manors, but only on a piecemeal basis. The only older road map was Ogilby's *Britannia* of 1675, which traced the routes of the main roads of England, only one of which was in Derbyshire. Clearly, travellers before this date needed to use other means of navigation, a topic dealt with in the next chapter.

Burdett's map, which was revised and updated in 1791, shows turnpike roads with double solid lines and other roads as double broken lines, but it does not mark minor roads or paths. The value of this survey is that it shows, for instance, that stretches of the Roman road north of Pikehall were still in use in the late eighteenth century, and so provides clues to the medieval road network. By comparing the detail on Burdett's map with early nineteenth-century maps such as George Sanderson's *Twenty Miles around Mansfield* (1835)[3] we can see the changes caused by the final development of the turnpike system and early industrialisation.

Large-scale maps are also a useful source of place names and road names. Settlement names such as Holloway, Cold Harbour and Stretton (meaning on the Roman street) offer useful clues. A good example of this is Shone and Smart's discussion of the Roman road south of Buxton:

> ... *there are a number of surviving 'Street' place names on the 1:25,000 OS map OL24. These are, from north to south: Street Farm at SK 1190 6745, Street House Farm at SK 1165 6740, Middle Street Farm at SK 1400 6518 and Straight Knolls Barn (= Street Knolls, Cameron, 1959) at SK 2256 5588.*[4]

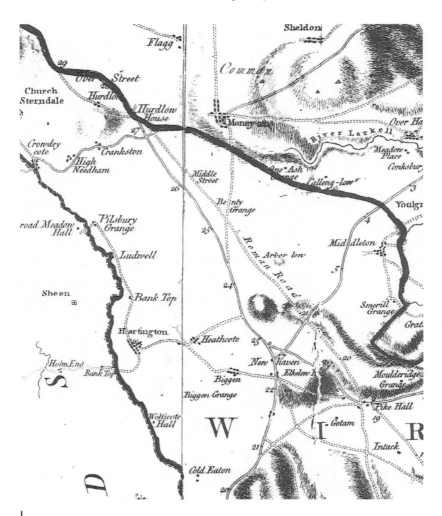

Burdett's map of NW Derbyshire, showing the Roman road.

Road names range from the obvious (Chesterfield Road) to the mysterious (Little London). The etymology of names must be approached with caution, but can be valuable and is discussed more fully below.

ROAD NAMES

With the arrival of Anglo-Saxon settlers from the late fifth century an early version of English began to be used for naming routes. The use of Celtic and then Latin has left little trace in terms of place and road names. The common Anglo-Saxon word for a road was 'way' (*Weg* in modern German). From this we have highway, byway, right of way, wayfarer and waymark. Some other terms for naming routes, in no particular order, are:

Street
Street was originally used to name the old Roman roads.

Gate
This was used by later Scandinavian settlers instead of 'way'. Note Saltergate, Glumangate and others in Chesterfield. But in more recent names 'gate' may refer to a turnpike tollgate, as at Ambergate.

Lane
This is generally used for minor routes.

Road
The etymology of this is confused, and one theory is that it derives from 'rode' i.e. something traversed on horseback. 'Road' came into general use only in the seventeenth century.

Causey or Causeway
This relates to a route paved with stone slabs for packhorse traffic, about two feet wide. Such routes were often on land liable to seasonal flooding, with a raised surface, as with the Causeway at Matlock.

Section of causey on public footpath between Whatstandwell and Crich.

Path

In fields or on moorland, a path is generally unfenced and has stiles at field boundaries. It may have always been a pedestrian route, or in places it may mark the route of a road which has gone out of use by vehicles.

For more details concerning Derbyshire road names see Appendix 1.

FURTHER READING

The pioneering study in this area was Dodd and Dodd's *Peakland Roads and Trackways* (1974, second edition 1980), which is still an invaluable source. David Hey's *Packmen, Carriers and Packhorse Roads* (2001) looks more closely at the kinds of products transported, and takes in south Yorkshire as well as north Derbyshire. Howard Smith's *Guide Stoops of Derbyshire* (1996, second edition 2009) and Neville Sharpe's *Crosses of the Peak District* (2002) are both valuable references to these roadside features. The first book to deal solely with the Portway was Cyril Spencer's *Walking the Derbyshire Portway* (1993), still a useful guide. Finally, J.B. Firth's *Highways and Byways in Derbyshire* (1905) is a fascinating account of the county's roads a century ago, and can be found quite cheaply.

It is more difficult to suggest sources for the national history of roads. Some are scholarly with a narrow focus, while others are very general. Overall, works which examine the details of road layouts in particular areas tend to be less interesting when the area is unfamiliar to the reader. Christopher Taylor's *Roads and Tracks of Britain* (1979) is comprehensive, though it is difficult to agree with all his views. But two rather dated though very readable works are Sir William Addison's *The Old Roads of England* (1980) and, with an emphasis on travellers, Thomas Burke's *Travel in England* (1942). There are many studies of Roman roads, but a good basic introduction is provided by Hugh Davies' *Roman Roads in Britain* (2008) in the Shire Archaeology series.

1

Prehistoric Routes

The northern part of Derbyshire has never been easy country to travel through. Even today, steep-sided valleys and winding roads can make for slow driving. The main national north-south highways find better routes, on either side of the Peak District. Inevitably, this topography has not produced rich farming country; in fact, historically Derbyshire was one of the poorest English counties. Much of the land is permanent pasture or moorland for grazing, and in the absence of intensive agriculture this has meant that there has been relatively little disturbance of ancient features such as burial sites or standing stones. Some, of course, have been lost, and there is documentary evidence of the deliberate destruction of prehistoric monuments by landowners, for religious or economic reasons. However, in comparison with lowland counties Derbyshire preserves quite a rich heritage of pre-Roman monuments such as stone circles and tumuli.

THE EARLY LANDSCAPE

It is difficult to know how different the Derbyshire landscape would have been in Neolithic (New Stone Age) times, about six thousand years ago. This was the period when people first began farming, probably by herding sheep and cows, and perhaps later growing some cereal crops. This was the beginning of settled habitation, in contrast to the nomadic life of the previous hunter-gatherers. It seems likely that river valleys were choked with dense wild woodland, while the hilltops might have supported lighter woodland giving way to open grassland in places where men had started clearing the tree cover. Herdsmen (or women) may have moved their animals to higher pastures in summer, thus retaining a semi-nomadic lifestyle, and hunting, especially in winter, would still provide an important source of food. There is evidence from a site near Parwich to support this view:

> By the Bronze Age, Dimbleby concluded, the hilltops were open pastures where limited cereal cultivation was practised, but patches of woodland and scrub, much as today, grew nearby. Thus tracts of upland may have been exposed by the Later Mesolithic period, but the valleys were in all probability still thickly wooded.[5]

It is generally assumed that the very first tracks were made by wild animals, in search of food or water, and that these were then used by hunters. Then, when settlements sprang up (which would also have been on the higher ground), these paths were modified into a network linking the farmsteads together. Clearly a prehistoric landscape of farms, moors, woods and ceremonial sites needed roads for many of the same reasons that we do today, both for local and everyday traffic as well as long-distance travel.

WHO WAS TRAVELLING?

An assumption is often made that because pre-modern communities were mainly self-sufficient, people rarely travelled, due to the difficulty of movement. This conclusion seems dubious for several reasons. In the first place, their ancestors had all been nomadic and thus their material culture encompassed the need to move regularly. Secondly, people have always understood that trade is essential for creating wealth. Finally, certain key goods were simply not available everywhere, and so trading routes were necessary. Examples of these include salt, from coastal salt pans, stone and flint from various sources including the Lake District, and later metals (or ores) such as copper and lead.

It is worth remembering (on the basis of archaeological finds of horse bits and similar) that horses were first domesticated in Britain about 2000 BCE,[6] during the Bronze Age. By the late Bronze Age wheeled vehicles were in use, but it seems unlikely that these were often found in the Peak District. A horse and rider can travel at about four miles per hour (mph) over long distances, and cover up to 30 miles a day, but of course we have no idea how widespread horse ownership was, and most travellers were probably on foot. On poor roads a walker can cover about two miles per hour, and perhaps 15 miles per day if fit. The Roman legions may have moved faster, but they were generally marching on well-surfaced roads. These practical limits on daily travelling distances applied, of course, right up to the mid-eighteenth century, when better roads permitted longer stages. Nevertheless, it is noteworthy (in an age when a weekend in New York is feasible for Londoners) that for many thousands of years before about 1800 CE few people had travelled at more than 10 mph or moved more than 30 miles in a day.

Travellers in this period would have included the packhorse men who made a living transporting scarce bulky commodities such as salt and metal ores, and probably merchants carrying more exotic items

Standing stone opposite the Malt Shovel pub, east of Wirksworth

imported from the continent, as have been found in the excavations of local burial sites. It seems likely that, as in the later medieval period, there were both specialist traders, always on the move and presumably with a good knowledge of the routes, and more local travellers such as farmers driving beasts to a market or herding animals to and from seasonal pasture, or just families visiting relatives. There would have been migrants seeking fresh opportunities in uncultivated areas, and possibly officials of the local chief. Pilgrims had to travel to ritual sites such as Arbor Low for ceremonies connected with the seasons of the year. Most road use would presumably have been seasonal, since long-distance travel in winter weather must have been arduous.

NAVIGATION

As mentioned above, many travellers would have been familiar with their routes through repeated journeying. But there must have been some system of marking long-distance tracks for the benefit of newcomers or strangers. Anyone who has ever tried to find their way in unfamiliar countryside through a maze of paths, sheep tracks and bridleways, even with the help of a good map, will sympathise with the problems early travellers faced in the same situation, but without the map. Christopher Taylor is dismissive of the difficulty: 'Indeed we do these prehistoric people a grave injustice in even conceiving that they needed such help to find their way across a country which must have been as familiar to them as our towns and villages are to us'.[7]

Yet given that all roads were unsurfaced, the difficulty for strangers in distinguishing between a track to the nearest farmyard and the way to the Lake District must have been formidable. In a pre-literate society only two solutions could have been employed. Either travellers memorised a series of distinctive natural

Standing stone west of Wirksworth on the Brassington road.

landmarks, which they used to orientate themselves, or else a series of man-made route markers, like waymarks on modern footpaths, were used to distinguish the 'highway'. These would most likely have been standing stones or cairns, supplemented subsequently by stone crosses and later still by milestones.

It is not clear whether tumuli or barrows were deliberately located beside long-distance roads, as Roman burials certainly were. A number can still be found alongside the route of the Portway, though this may be coincidental. However, Bill Bevan, writing of a barrow in the upper Derwent Valley, says:

> *This barrow was designed to be seen by people moving across the landscape, maybe placed to identify traditional claims to hunting grounds or seasonal pastures... These were places which may have been shared pastures for surrounding settlements at lower altitudes.*[8]

It has long been thought that the earliest long-distance routes were ridgeways. A number of examples in southern Britain are regularly mentioned, such as the Icknield Way running northeast into East Anglia, or the Berkshire Ridgeway. Taylor has argued that such routes may not be prehistoric, and that the apparent clustering of prehistoric monuments along their course may be coincidental, for high land is less intensively farmed today and therefore features such as barrows tend to survive better. While it may be true that at some periods in prehistory the population density was high enough to require the clearance of lower, heavier soils, it still seems reasonable to assume that long-distance travel at the time was mainly along upland routes.

There were several valid reasons for this preference for ridgeways. Not only was the higher ground less thickly wooded, but also by keeping to the heights travellers were saved the effort of climbing in and out of marshy, overgrown valleys. While there would clearly have to be river crossings in some places, where fords were established, the need for these was kept to a minimum. In addition, navigation was made easier by enabling travellers to orientate themselves on distant landmarks. Furthermore, such ridgeways allowed travellers a better view of possible dangers ahead, such as robbers or dangerous animals. When the time came to make camp for the night, high ground offered a more secure camping site, as will be discussed below.

THE DERBYSHIRE PORTWAY

'Portway' is an Anglo-Saxon name which was apparently given by the Saxons to some older, pre-Roman roads. There are various portways in England, for example between Southampton and Northampton, or the route from Silchester to Salisbury, but there is no agreement on the meaning of the name. One common suggestion is that it means 'road to a market'. But this makes little sense, as markets were not common until the thirteenth century, and in any case the Derbyshire Portway does not link market towns.

It seems more likely that the 'port' refers to a shelter or 'harbour' where travellers could spend the night. Clearly, in an age before inns, overnight security would be a major problem for long-distance travellers. They needed a defensive enclosure where they could cook, graze their animals and sleep without threats from wild beasts or robbers. (The same function was provided until recently by *caravanserai* in the Middle East.) There are a number of sites along the Portway's route, vaguely called 'hillforts', which could have been defended by wooden palisades. Two of these are called Arbour Hill (Wollaton Park and Dale) and another is Harborough Rocks (above Wirksworth). Table 1 shows their distribution along the route, and also their fairly regular spacing.

TABLE 1. APPROXIMATE DISTANCE BETWEEN SITES OF POSSIBLE 'PORTS' ON THE DERBYSHIRE PORTWAY. SOURCE: AUTHOR'S COMPILATION.

Trent river port, Colwick area	
	4 miles
Arbour Hill, Wollaton Park	
	6.5 miles
Arbour Hill, Dale	
	6 miles
Horsley Castle	
	8 miles
Alport Height	
	6.5 miles
Harborough Rocks	
	6 miles

Cratcliff Rocks	
	7 miles
Fin Cop	
	9 miles
Man Tor	
	9 miles
Snake Inn area	

While these places could have been used as strongholds by local tribes in times of war (as seems likely at Fin Cop, for instance), they would have had more regular use as early inns, with perhaps a local custodian charging travellers for water and supplies.

Cratcliff Rocks, Harthill Moor.

The route of the Derbyshire Portway was first suggested by the eminent local historian R.W.P. Cockerton (1904–80). He was a Bakewell solicitor who was an expert on the Roman period in Derbyshire, being involved in many excavations. He published a series of articles in the *Derbyshire Countryside* between 1932 and 1936 (see Appendix 2) which set out his thesis. His starting point was the existence of a string of 'port' place names, such as Alport and Alport Height, which mark a line running from the northwest to the southeast across the county. On the map these seem to be linked by a credible route, although there are sections where this is unclear. (Hey[9] maintains that the place name evidence for the Portway is unconvincing, but does not explain why.) Secondly, there are references in medieval documents such as charters to a 'Portawaye', often used to define land boundaries. Finally, Cockerton pointed to the physical existence of tracks and paths which preserve a right of way along the possible route and allow most of it to be followed today.

Cockerton had a formidable knowledge of the history of Derbyshire roads, and his articles deal with different sections of the Portway, from the north around Wardlow to the Derbyshire/Nottinghamshire border at Sandiacre. Subsequent historians of Peak District roads such as Dodd and Dodd (1980 [1974]) have accepted Cockerton's thesis without attempting to establish the Portway's purpose or likely route beyond the county. In any case, such discussion is highly speculative, since all road systems evolve continually to meet changing needs.

The economic life of the Peak District has fluctuated significantly with climatic and other changes over the last six thousand years, with marked periods of recession and depopulation. At different times the Portway might have carried lead ore from the mines near Wirksworth, groups of migrants or invaders, and pagan or Christian pilgrims. All would be using it as a convenient route from the river systems of eastern England into the northwest. Today there seems to be a widespread acceptance among local historians that there was a Portway running northwest through the county, but little agreement about its age or even its approximate route.

Nottingham was for many centuries the head of navigation on the River Trent; a bridge was recorded there as early as 924 CE,[10] and this would have been the usual upper limit for sea-going vessels. Therefore a possible destination (or starting point) for the Portway could have been near Nottingham. Recently I have tried to establish a likely route from the Hemlock Stone (my previous end point on the Portway) to downstream of Trent Bridge, and this is given in more detail in Chapter 8. It is noteworthy that the route seems to have passed close by Lenton Priory, a major religious establishment of the twelfth century, and home to an important annual autumn fair.

At the northern end of the route, Mam Tor seems to have been another fortified site for travellers, since it is hard to imagine that, at an altitude of 500 metres, it was permanently inhabited. From there a possible extension is via Nether Booth and up the Woodlands Valley to the Snake Pass. Confusingly, there is an Alport Dale branching off this valley to the north, which leads to the rocks of Alport Castles. But this dale is a dead end, while the Roman road over the Snake Pass led to a fort near Glossop, so it seems unlikely that the pre-Roman route would have taken a different path.

It is impossible to specify the date when the Portway would have come into use, but it may be linked to the remarkable growth of population which occurred in the Peak District between 2000 and 1000 BCE. According to Richard Hodges, this happened as a result of a period of climate warming which led to summers being 2–3°C warmer than they are now. Remarkably, it has been estimated that parts of the area had a population similar to that of today. This was the period, when Arbor Low was first constructed, which has left a rich archaeological legacy. Presumably both cereal cultivation and pasture for cattle were expanded to support the increase in numbers. But as cooling set in before 1000 BCE a process of depopulation began, especially on the East Moor.

Sanderson's map of Nottingham (1835) showing Sneinton Hermitage (lower centre)
and 'Druidical Remains' (upper centre).

There is a noticeable scarcity of Iron Age finds in the Peak District, which historians have explained by the abandonment of marginal land.

Parts of the Portway probably enabled the Romans to gain access to the region before they constructed their own road network. Their arrival certainly brought about a period of economic growth, both in terms of providing a market for agricultural produce and the development of mining, especially for lead. It seems likely that the Portway was used by the Saxons, and there is archaeological and written evidence of medieval and later use. Features such as the hermitages seem to have been in use in the thirteenth and fourteenth centuries, for example, while in the early eighteenth century, some sections were still used as a route from Derby to Manchester.

But in this later period significant changes began to alter the Derbyshire landscape and eventually led to the demise of the old road as a long-distance route. Enclosures, both private and parliamentary, brought about the end of the medieval system of open fields and common grazing on the moors, and caused the construction of the dense grid of dry-stone walls that now seems so characteristic of the area. (Some walls are much older, but the majority date to these enclosures.)

At the same time turnpike roads were constructed to speed up travel, and in order to maximise toll collection some older routes were closed to prevent traffic using them to avoid the toll bars. Crowhill Lane near Ashford is an example of this practice, being a replacement for the old route which would have by-passed the toll house. Simultaneously, the demands of an industrialising society led to the growth of large-scale quarrying and the rapid expansion of lead and coal mining in the region, as well as the construction of railways. All of these developments combined to obscure and in places obliterate the old route, so that by the nineteenth century it was only used for local traffic, although remarkably the name of the Portway survived in places, for example between Holbrook and Coxbench.

Over a period of several thousand years it cannot be expected that the exact line of the original route, if there ever was one, can be fully traced. There were certainly branch tracks which linked the Portway with major settlements both west and east, such as Chesterfield. Some of these routes are discussed in Chapter 9. Perhaps what is remarkable, given the huge time span involved, is that a considerable proportion of the route can still be followed on footpaths and green lanes. It may be that ultimately it is the walker who is best placed to judge the validity of this route as it was originally developed: to allow travellers on foot or horseback to pass through the Peak District as safely and speedily as possible.

2

Roman Roads

The subject of Roman roads has fascinated many people, and it is not hard to see why. Roads enter history for the first time in the Roman period, in that classical authors recount their experiences of travel around the Roman Empire. Their written records survive from various parts of Europe and the Near East, and it is reasonable to assume that some of these accounts could also apply to conditions of travel in Britain. The Romans used their formidable military authority to construct, for the first time, a system of roads across the whole of Europe using a fairly uniform pattern of construction. The primary purpose of this network was military control: it allowed troops to be marched rapidly to any uprising, and it also facilitated the rapid carriage of news and instructions, by means of relays of riders.

The poet Statius (c. 45–96 CE) has left an account of road construction in Italy. He describes the cutting of a wide trench, which was then refilled with foundation material, while kerbstones lined the edges. This created a raised bank known as an *aggar*. The surface was covered with stone slabs or gravel, while ditches on either side carried rainwater away. There is also evidence that soldiers were used for road building, probably to keep them occupied and fit.

Near to towns roads were often lined by tombs, since the Romans thought that the dead would be better remembered if travellers could read the funerary inscriptions. In more remote places there were roadside sanctuaries to the gods and also to the particular divinities of road junctions (e.g. *Quadruviae* for the meeting point of four roads). We do not know whether these customs were brought to Britain, but it appears that the basic principles of road surveying and building were followed everywhere, allowing for differences in the local availability of construction materials.

ROMAN ROADS IN DERBYSHIRE

Part of the appeal of Roman roads for historians, both amateur and professional, is that for the first time a planned network of (theoretically) straight roads covered the country. But it is worth remembering that they were built alongside an existing network of tracks which had long served the needs of the natives, and that in some cases these (non-straight) routes were adopted by the conquerors. Establishing the details of the local road network is surprisingly difficult in some areas, and much time has been spent discussing roads which 'should' have existed but probably never did.

For example, Dodd and Dodd's map of the Roman roads in the Peak District (in *Peakland Roads and Trackways*[11]) shows the 'conjectured' site of Lutudarum as near Carsington, joined to Chesterfield and Rocester by a road called Hereward Street. It also shows the continuation of The Street from Buxton crossing this road and heading southeast to Little Chester. But there is no real evidence that either of these roads

Excavations at Little Chester, Derby, 2016.

existed in Roman times. In fact, it has recently and convincingly been argued that The Street continued on to Wirksworth. (For an up-to-date summary of the situation see Shone and Ward [2017] on the website of the Wirksworth Archaeological Society.) Beyond that town the Romans may have used the Portway going southeast to Brackley Gate, at which point they could have joined Ryknild Street to reach Little Chester. In other words, the southern extension of The Street may never have existed.

Following the Emperor Claudius' successful invasion of Britain in 43 CE, the legions gradually worked their way north, consolidating defences, and reached the Midlands by about 70 CE. A small fort was established on the banks of the Derwent, first on the west side and later on the east bank, which was called Derventio and is now the site of Little Chester, a suburb of Derby. Although probably not continuously garrisoned after the frontier had moved north, it became the focus for a small civilian township.

William Stukeley's map of 1723 shows a ditched and walled site close to the river, with the Chesterfield to Lichfield road (called Ricning

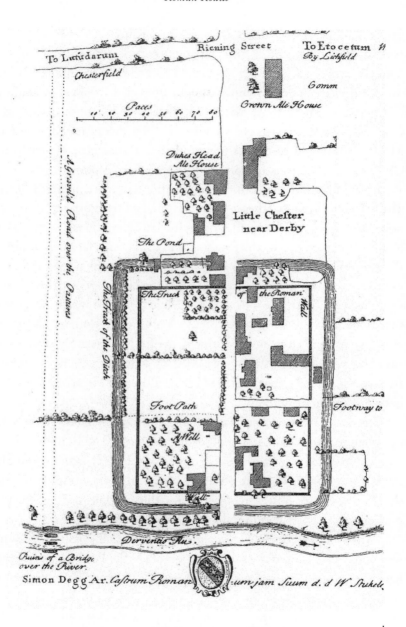

Plan of Little Chester, Derby by William Stukeley, 1723.

Street here) passing to the east. This was probably the most important part of the local network, and today its route southwest of Derby is marked by the A38, running almost straight towards Lichfield. To the west of the city another mainly straight line on the map is created by Long Lane, coming from Rocester, which is clearly aligned to Little Chester. The route north is also quite straight, except for the bend at Morley Moor, and continues (via a possible fortlet near Pentrich) to Chesterfield. (See Brassington [1981][12] for a full account.)

In the north of the county the situation is rather different. Both The Street, running southeast from Buxton, and the Portway, reaching northwest from Wirksworth, appear to be older routes, sections of which were upgraded by the Romans, and the latter is far from straight. Brough, in the Hope valley, was another fort, from where Batham Gate ran over the moors to Buxton, while the high-level Doctor's Gate went over the Snake Pass to a fort at Melandra. It is worth repeating that none of these names, except Derventio, were Roman, and even that may be derived from the Celtic name for the River Derwent. The situation in the Peak is fully discussed by Peter Wroe[13] in his paper *Roman Roads in the Peak District* (1982), although some of his claims have since been disputed.

The roads built or resurfaced by the Romans in Derbyshire were not intended to be main imperial roads, which could be 12 metres wide and had *mansios*, or rest houses, at regular intervals in order to supply fresh horses for messengers. Recent excavation near Minninglow has shown a width of only three metres for this section of The Street;[14] previous researchers had found a width of up to four metres.

After military control of the region had been achieved the Romans were anxious to exploit the mineral resources of the Peak, and lead 'pigs' have been found stamped with the letters 'LVT', short for Lutudarum, thought to be the local centre of lead production. Unfortunately there is no agreement about the location of this place, or even whether it was a town or a district. Claims have been made for both Chesterfield and

Wirksworth, but it seems likely that, as in the Middle Ages, mining was widely scattered and one reason for the construction or improvement of the northern routes was to facilitate lead production and transport. Most probably, what we now call Ryknild Street and Long Lane were built first for military purposes, and then when other roads (including some which are now lost) were needed for commercial use, these were either constructed from scratch, or were ancient tracks re-surfaced.

AFTER THE LEGIONS LEFT

Our modern road system is still marked by the legacy of the Roman network, and the roads they built continued in use for hundreds of years. However, in the absence of a strong central authority after 410 CE, road maintenance virtually ceased and the system gradually deteriorated. Bridges would be washed away by floods, culverts could become blocked, and fallen trees might obstruct the way. The surface paving stones would offer a tempting quarry for building materials. Moreover, as town life diminished, there was no longer such a need to link these centres of activity. As a result, while short sections continued in use, long-distance travel tended to revert to the older routes.

Examples of this can be seen by looking at Burdett's 1791 map. Between Little Chester and Oakerthorpe, over fairly low-lying land, there is virtually no trace left of the Roman Ryknild Street. In comparison, on the high limestone plateau to the north of Derbyshire, a lengthy section of The Street running north of Pikehall is shown as being still in use (see p. xviii).

3

Pre-Conquest Derbyshire

Between the end of Roman rule around 410 and the Norman Conquest in 1066 there is very little documentary evidence of the conditions of travel in England. This is especially true of Derbyshire, which remained relatively isolated, and as a result there has been much speculation in an attempt to fill the lacuna. Earlier historians imagined a dramatic scenario, as waves of Saxon invaders drove the apparently helpless British natives into the western hills, along with much plundering and pillaging. But this lurid picture has become discredited and the impact of Saxon culture is now seen as more gradual and small-scale, especially in agriculturally marginal areas such as the Peak. Yet even in these districts the Early English language came into general use, so that with few exceptions (e.g. Crich, Pentrich and Pennyunk Lane above Ashford) all place and road names in Derbyshire are now of Anglo-Saxon rather than Celtic origin.

Leslie Alcock[15] sees trade and travel in Anglo-Saxon England as being almost entirely local:

Within the framework of a farming economy this [a day's walk] was probably the limit of trade, or indeed of movement at all, except for certain necessities with a naturally limited distribution like salt and iron.

But a more recent view is expressed by Francis Pryor:[16]

Maybe it is because we have tended to look at permanent structures, such as great buildings, barrows, town walls and so forth that archaeologists – and I include prehistorians in this – have generally underestimated the extent to which the population of Britain and western Europe moved around. We know that pottery and coins moved, and we also know that styles of art and decoration spread across Europe very rapidly. But we do not then go on to say that people themselves must have moved too. Just because pre-Roman roads have left little trace, some prehistorians seem to believe that they were not used.

What is conventionally (and unhelpfully) called The Dark Ages spans a period of over six hundred years, and for much of that time people must have been getting on with their normal lives, with only the occasional Saxon, Viking or English army marching past down the old roads. At the same time, there were clearly plagues, climatic changes and other natural phenomena which may have caused recession and led to roads falling into further disrepair.

DERBYSHIRE AND DANELAW

In this context it is worth summarising what is known about Derbyshire in this period. Repton in south Derbyshire was an important site,

The crypt of St Wystan's Church, Repton.

lying close to the Trent, which must have been a significant transport route. The Mercian king was first baptised there in the mid-seventh century, and in the eighth century the church's crypt was constructed as a burial place for the royal family. But soon afterwards the bishop's seat was moved to Lichfield, and in 873–4 a Viking army, which had presumably sailed up the Trent, over-wintered near Repton, causing significant damage to the buildings.

Other early Christian sites are marked by stone carvings, some of which have survived better than their churches (most Saxon buildings being replaced post-Conquest). There are fine carved crosses at Eyam, Bakewell and Hope, which may have been used to preach from in the early days of missionary work, not to mention the outstanding Wirksworth Stone, a richly carved coffin lid dating from about 800 CE. So we can assume that Christianity had spread into the Peak District by the seventh century, and it has even been claimed (on place name evidence) that Christian communities may have existed in late Roman times in areas such as Wirksworth. A royal refugee from Northumbria, Alkmund, was killed at Derby (or Northworthy, to use its Saxon name)

The ninth-century Wirksworth Stone in St Mary's Church.

in 800 and was soon canonised. Today his intricately carved coffin can be seen in Derby Museum. The quality of all this work, which must represent only a fraction of what once existed, given the iconoclasm of the Civil War period, suggests the existence of skilled travelling craftsmen at the time.

From about 880 Derbyshire was subject to Viking rule as part of the Danelaw, whose capital was at York. In the mid-tenth century we get the first mention of 'wapentakes', an administrative division of the county into six parts. (Outside the Danelaw these are called 'hundreds'.) They seem to have met monthly to settle disputes, impose taxation and deal with other civil matters. The meeting points may have been linked to their names, so the Morleyston and Litchurch wapentake would have met somewhere near Morley (see Chapter 8C). Parallel to the creation of wapentakes may have been the development of parishes, the smallest ecclesiastical unit. Initially parishes were centred on minster churches such as Duffield and Ashbourne, and were far larger than the size of modern parishes. The boundaries for these divisions into shires, wapentakes and parishes tended to use natural

Stone sarcophagus, believed to be St Alkmund's, Derby Museum.

markers, notably streams and rivers, but in some cases old tracks such as the Portway were employed.

Considerable road traffic must have been created by the participants at the wapentakes and the congregations of the local minster churches, for both masses and funerals. There is also evidence of two kinds of pilgrimage in this period. Firstly, visits to the shrine of a local saint (St Chad at Lichfield was popular, but St Alkmund must also have been venerated, as was St Wystan at Repton). Secondly, for wealthier people there were long-distance pilgrimages to Rome and the continental or Irish monasteries. Diana Webb[17] points out that Bede mentions certain English kings making several Roman visits from the late seventh century.

The minster churches may have been the focus of settlements, but in general most people continued to live in scattered farmsteads, and villages were only formed in the latter part of this period, according to place name evidence. Lead continued to be the most significant product of Derbyshire. Dorothy Whitelock[18] mentions that in 835 'Wirksworth was rendering annually to the Archbishop of Canterbury lead to the value of 300 shillings', though unfortunately we do not know how or where it was delivered.

None of this suggests a population that was rooted to the spot. Whether for trade, spiritual or legal concerns, substantial numbers must have been on the move, despite the dangers and difficulties involved, and using roads that were probably no worse than they had been in the Iron Age. While we have no knowledge of how they were maintained (as is true of many aspects of life at this time) we do know that certain improvements were made; for example, the first bridge over the Trent at Nottingham was built in 924 by Edward the Elder. We can assume that parts of the Roman network remained in use, and may have been repaired on an ad hoc basis, while the older native British tracks, now called portways, would probably have provided the main arteries for travel.

4

Travel 1066–1700

Although this lengthy timespan covers the High Middle Ages, the Dissolution of the Monasteries, the Reformation, the Civil War, the Restoration and the Glorious Revolution, there were few major changes in the technology of roads or travel during this time, although clearly it spans various periods of economic recession and growth. The first turnpike roads appeared in the late seventeenth century, but were not significant until the next century. Surprisingly, it is estimated that the population of England in 1700, at about 5,200,000, was little higher than its pre-Black Death level in 1348 (4,810,000).[19] In 1600 the population of Derbyshire is estimated at about 70,000, which was somewhat lower than in 1290.

CROSSING THE DERWENT: FORDS AND BRIDGES

Today we tend to take bridges for granted. Driving at speed, a driver is barely aware that a sizeable river is being crossed. But a thousand years ago rivers, especially the Derwent, posed a formidable barrier to travellers in Derbyshire. Now the river levels are checked by the dams in the northern Derwent valley and other flood-control measures, but in the past water levels rose and fell much more sharply. The first river crossings were fords, located where the river widened and ran shallower, and where a rider could often cross without getting too wet, and also where cattle could be driven over. But when water levels rose in winter, especially for pedestrians, fords could easily become impassable.

Place names on the Derwent, from north to south, such as Hazelford, Grindleford, Cromford, Homesford and Milford, indicate sites of fords, and it is worth noting that although Matlock Bridge dates from the thirteenth century, the bridge at Milford was only constructed in the late eighteenth century, by the Strutts of Belper. Burdett's map shows a ford over the Derwent near Duffield, which was approached on the Makeney side by Save Penny Lane: presumably the price of the toll at Duffield Bridge. At Holme Bridge over the Wye above Bakewell the ford can still be seen next to the packhorse bridge, which was built in 1664.

Fords and bridges were a critical part of the road network; often they were places where several routes came together to take advantage of a safe crossing, as at Cromford, where the roads to Starkholmes and Lea join on the east bank. Simple bridges may have existed before the Romans, and were certainly being constructed in Saxon times. The earliest would consist of stone pillars with a wooden decking, vulnerable to destruction by winter floods. In the Middle Ages some of these were replaced by more substantial arched stone structures: more expensive to build but much more resilient. Yet timber bridges survived until quite late in places. For example,

Holme Bridge, over the River Wye upstream from Bakewell.

Yorkshire Bridge below Ashopton was wooden until 1695, when the Quarter Sessions allocated £130 to rebuild it in stone. Because of repeated rebuilding and widening it can be difficult to say when a bridge was first constructed at a certain site. However, Alport Bridge on the Lathkill was built in 1718 at the command of the Quarter Sessions, as the ford was becoming impassable due to heavy traffic on the Portway, while Whatstandwell Bridge can be dated to an agreement of 1390 between the Abbot of Darley and John de Stepul, who had offered to pay for the work.

Early stone bridges were of two widths: packhorse bridges just wide enough for a laden train, with low parapets to avoid snagging the panniers, and bridges broad enough for a cart to cross. The latter were obviously more expensive to construct and were only found in areas where gentler gradients allowed carriage by cart or waggon. Packhorse bridges still survive in parts of the Peak, such as on the River Bradford at Youlgrave. Cart bridges have generally been widened more recently

Packhorse Bridge on the River Bradford at Youlgrave.

to take two-way traffic, but One Arch Bridge below Chatsworth Park is still restricted to a single traffic lane and gives an idea of the dimensions of older bridges.

The skill involved in building an arched stone bridge was considerable, and masons with the necessary skills may have been peripatetic, moving from site to site. The cost of the work was also substantial, and it was often borne by a bequest, or by a nearby monastery or priory, which would have an interest in making travel easier. Chapels were sometimes built near or on bridges to allow travellers to pray for a safe journey, and to give offerings for the upkeep of the structure. Two examples in Derbyshire are at St Mary's Bridge in Derby and the ruined chapel at Cromford Bridge (west bank). In some cases a toll was charged for crossing: Halfpenny Bridge at Ambergate is a late example from 1792.

Severe winter floods were a constant threat. Rebuilding the bridge at Belper in 1798 cost £2,220, while ten years earlier St Mary's Bridge

Chapel on St Mary's Bridge, Derby.

in Derby had cost £4,000 to rebuild. Bridges were also at risk from heavy loads, so that in 1500 carrying millstones over Baslow Bridge was prohibited, with a fine of six shillings for offenders.

The difficulty in determining the location of early river crossings can be seen in the case of Matlock. According to Lynn Willies,[20] the Domesday settlement of Mestesforde may not have been around the present site of Matlock Bridge, which was built in 1250. He presents evidence to suggest that the ford may have been half a mile downstream, where Pic Tor Lane drops down from Old Matlock, on a route that would have linked up with Salters Lane on Masson Hill opposite. This would explain why the urban focus of Matlock continued to be around St Giles Church, rather than the town bridge, until the nineteenth century.

In his recent study of the importance of bridges to the medieval road system David Harrison[21] concludes:

The principal findings … at most locations where there was a bridge in 1750 there had been one in the thirteenth century and at many locations there had been a bridge in 1100 – probably mirror the fundamental continuities in the economy over this period. This suggests how much the pre-industrial economy of the seventeenth century had in common with the late medieval or even the eleventh-century economy. The findings also demonstrate the capacity of medieval society to invest very heavily in practical civil engineering projects.

THE TRADITION OF PILGRIMAGE

Pilgrimage existed in the ancient classical world and it is likely that pagan Britain had pilgrims who visited sacred wells, groves or burial sites. The essence of pilgrimage is a journey to a significant place, where the pilgrim benefits from closeness to spiritual power. These places were often remote and inaccessible, such as mountain tops or islands. It was also thought that the burial place of a spiritual or temporal leader would be of value to the visitor, while in the Christian period the focus was often on a religious relic, such as a saint's bone or a fragment of the holy cross.

Pilgrim figure, All Saints
Church, Youlgrave

Although regional and international pilgrimage was already undertaken in Saxon Britain, with the arrival of the larger monasteries such as the Benedictines after the Conquest, national pilgrimage became more widespread, perhaps peaking between 1100 and 1400. One of the best-known works of early English literature, Geoffrey Chaucer's *Canterbury Tales*, was written around 1388. Despite being a work of fiction, it clearly had some basis in fact, and portrays a cross-section of society taking part in a pilgrimage for a variety of motives, both religious and secular.

Among Chaucer's 30 travellers who had banded together, partly for security, on the road to Canterbury were five with experience of international travel (Knight, Squire, Shipman, Pardoner and Wife of Bath). Such foreign journeys were expensive, and none of Chaucer's pilgrims were peasants, who formed the bulk of the population. But it is likely that the latter might make local, one-day pilgrimages to a nearby shrine, and for similar reasons. The commonest motives for making a pilgrimage were to seek a cure for a medical problem, to make penance for a sin or crime, to take part in a seasonal ritual such as the local patron saint's day, or simply as a holiday trip. As Chaucer wrote: '[in April] … then people long to go on pilgrimages'.[22]

As mentioned in the previous chapter, local saints such as St Bertram at Ilam or St Alkmund at Derby would have attracted pilgrims in pre-Conquest times, but the medieval monasteries such as Dale (dedicated to St Mary) and the rebuilt minster churches tended to have more cosmopolitan patron saints. Larger monasteries kept guest houses for travellers, and also helped to maintain local roads and bridges. Wayside crosses, as are still found in Catholic parts of Europe such as Bavaria, often marked the way to a nearby shrine. A rare local survivor is Wheston Cross near Tideswell, whose remote location probably helped protect it from the puritan destruction of the sixteenth century. One side of the carved head shows the Madonna and child, the other depicts the crucifixion. Such crosses would have had the dual function of waymark and prayer station. Eyam Cross is an earlier example, possibly dating from the eighth century. Another feature of medieval wayfaring was the many hermits who led a solitary existence in remote caves but nevertheless scraped a living by guiding travellers on their journey. The existence of four hermitages on the route of the Portway (see Chapter 8) is a striking example of this.

By the sixteenth century Protestant theology was gaining ground and the belief in the power of relics was beginning to fade, while the monks had lost some of their original zeal. The Dissolution of the Monasteries in 1539 signalled an end to the age of pilgrimage, so there was no-one now willing to maintain bridges or provide hospitality for travellers. Not only were shrines and relics lost, but objects such as carved crosses were destroyed in the iconoclastic wave that continued beyond the Civil War a century later. However, it seems likely that small-scale, local pilgrimages may have continued, and the continued

Eighth-century cross, Eyam churchyard.

popularity of John Bunyan's *Pilgrim's Progress* for centuries after its initial publication in 1678 suggests a resilient interest in the topic. It can be argued that the enthusiasm for attending spas and 'hydros', which began at about the same time, is effectively a secularisation of the tradition of pilgrimage; in fact there is evidence that Bath, the premier English spa, was a site of healing during the Iron Age. Matlock Bath was initially developed for visitors in 1698 with the construction of the first bath house; a topic that will be explored in the next two chapters.

ROAD MAINTENANCE

Even in a relatively remote area like Derbyshire there was an increase in road traffic as the economy grew in the period known as the High Middle Ages (1100–1300). One indication of this is the granting of market charters, starting with Hartington in 1203, Chesterfield a year later, Bakewell in 1254 and Wirksworth in 1306. By this time most people lived within seven miles of a market, which was regarded as close enough to make the journey there and back in a day.

While markets were held weekly and might include the sale of both produce and livestock, fairs were annual, and would draw traders and customers from a wider radius. Many Derbyshire fairs began in the thirteenth century (Ilkeston in 1252, Ashbourne in 1297), but it is unlikely that these would match the eleven days of the Lenton Fair held just outside Nottingham at Lenton Priory, where a charter of 1252 gave the monks the right to hold a fair in November. Indeed, the Lenton Fair continued long after the Dissolution, right up to the twentieth century, having by then evolved into a horse fair (see Chapter 8A).

The growth of trading, exemplified by the development of both markets and fairs, would have created more road traffic and put a fragile network under great strain. The Statute of Winchester in 1285 ordered the clearance of undergrowth on either side of main roads throughout the country to deter robbery, and also sought to put responsibility for road maintenance on the manors, although it is uncertain how effective either measure was. During this period, the devolution of responsibility for roads either to the manor or to the parish was liable to failure, since at this local level there were neither the necessary skills nor interest in the condition of the major highways.

It is difficult to establish the real state of medieval roads, though the conventional picture is that they were in a poor condition. As Thomas Burke[23] claimed:

> *If, in a tempest, trees fell and barred the way, it was nobody's business to remove them. Heavy rains invariably flooded the roads and turned them into quagmires full of pot holes and pools in which a man might drown.*

On the other hand, some recent writers such as Dorian Gerhold[24] have argued that the state of the roads was generally adequate for the demands of the traffic. Certainly trade increased over the period, and many journeys were completed without suffering accidents. There was a great difference between roads on clay soils, such as near London, and those on limestone or chalk, which drained much better. What is certain, however, is the slowness of travel: the Cavendish family's annual removal from Hardwick Hall to their London house took five days.

In 1555 the Statute of Labour attempted to improve the situation by requiring all parishes to elect a Highway Surveyor on an annual basis to organise road repair. Every householder was expected to give four (later six) days' unpaid work to maintain local roads, and those with horses and carts were expected to provide these for free. Inevitably, the post of Surveyor was unpopular, as no-one wanted the responsibility, and nor would they have knowledge of the skills of road building. Another flaw in the system was that some parishes had more, and busier, roads than others. Yet however imperfect, the system remained in operation for nearly three hundred years, and evidence from Mathew Gibbons' diary (see Chapter 6) shows it still operating in Rowsley in the eighteenth century.

ROAD VEHICLES

Packhorse trains were probably the commonest means of moving goods a long distance from prehistoric times through into the early modern period, with some routes surviving into the nineteenth century. The cargo was generally carried in panniers on either side of the animal, which might also have been a pony or mule. Each could carry up to two-and-a-half hundredweight, so that a train of 40 animals would transport five tons of salt or ore. Two men known as 'jaggers' would accompany the train, a term commemorated by Jaggers Lane east of Matlock. There are still two Derbyshire pubs called *The Packhorse*,

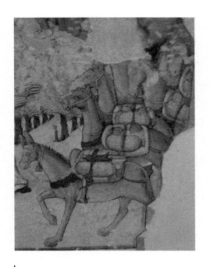

Fresco painting of packhorses, Seville, Spain.

one at Crowdecote and another at Little Longstone. Despite being such a common sight for thousands of years, there are few surviving pictures of the trains; the example here is from San Isidoro Monastery near Seville in Spain – note the bell on the lead horse.

The great advantage of the packhorse was flexibility. Although a horse and cart could carry a ton and only needed one driver, the packhorse could use the narrowest of tracks and bridges and moved quickly over long distances, even in hill country such as north Derbyshire. Although light and valuable loads were most efficient, packhorses carried anything that could be fitted into panniers, including coal and lime. One regular route brought cotton goods from Manchester to Nottingham, and returned laden with malt.

For farm work and local trade both carts and wains (two wheels) and waggons (four) were in use in this period, being especially suitable for moving bulky items such as timber and stone. Oxen were often used to pull waggons, but horses gradually superseded them. David Hey's research,[25] partly using probate inventories, shows that wheeled vehicles were used throughout northern Derbyshire and southern Yorkshire during this period. But the simplest form of goods transport was by sledge, which didn't require the wheelwright's skill. One reminder of this is Sledgegate Lane at Lea Green, which would have given local farmers access to the moor.

CHURCH PATHS

In medieval Britain burial in consecrated ground was an important requirement for future salvation. There were fewer churchyards licensed for burial available then, since parishes were generally larger and settlement was more dispersed. Consequently, coffins often had to be carried long distances. The villagers of Edale, for instance, had to carry their dead to the churchyard at Hope, involving a steep climb over the ridge below Mam Tor, with Hollins Cross marking the spot where the bearers would rest after the climb or before starting the descent on either side. These routes from outlying hamlets and farms to the nearest licensed church were sometimes called coffin paths, lych ways, or burial roads, although clearly they were also used by local people attending regular church services.

Footpath to Horsley church from the Coxbench-Holbrook road.

Many of the older churches in Derbyshire stand at the centre of a network of paths radiating out from the churchyard such as at Horsley, where five paths converge. Other examples are Ashover, Morley, Crich and Bonsall. There is a particularly well-defined path running over the ridge between Little Eaton and Holbrook, leading to Duffield Bridge and the adjacent church. Today, of course, these paths have simply become part of the footpath network, and their origins are mainly forgotten.

A considerable folklore is attached to these church paths, especially in western parts of Britain such as Wales and the Lake District. Their regular use by the dead gave the routes a special significance, almost as if they were extensions of the churchyard itself.

As Puck says in *A Midsummer Night's Dream*:[26]

Now it is the time of night,
That the graves, all gaping wide,
Every one lets forth his sprite,
In the church-way paths to glide.

5

The Turnpike Era: 1700–1840

The basic principle of turnpike roads was to shift responsibility for road maintenance from the parish to the road users, who paid in proportion to the wear and tear they inflicted. Despite a rather shaky start, the development of a network of turnpike roads did eventually permit faster and more comfortable journeys, and also played a part in the economic expansion of the eighteenth century, which was one consequence of the political stability created by the constitutional settlement of 1688.

Yet despite their value, turnpikes were never popular: the principle of free use of the King's Highway was too firmly established in popular belief, and in many areas of Britain there was low-level conflict with the turnpike trusts, both in terms of vandalism and attempts to evade payment. Moreover, the early turnpikes mainly followed existing

Milestone on the Bakewell-
Ashbourne turnpike near Winster.

routes and provided minimal improvements for travellers; it was only after 1750 that more scientific attempts were made to improve road surfacing and to construct new routes with easier gradients.

Another difficulty was that turnpike trusts had to borrow heavily for the initial expense of setting up toll gates and toll houses, as well as to cover the costs of road repair and wages. Yet the income from tolls was rarely enough to cover running costs and repay the borrowing, and so, added to interest payments on the initial capital raised, they often went deeper into debt. Turnpike trusts had to be set up by Act of Parliament, and they were often controlled by local landowners and industrialists – such as the Duke of Devonshire or Richard Arkwright – who had an interest in improving transport. The trusts often auctioned the right to collect tolls, but they still had to employ surveyors, clerks and road menders. Travellers on foot were always exempt from payment, as were Royal Mail coaches.

DERBYSHIRE TURNPIKES

The first turnpike in the county, which was authorised in 1738, ran from Shardlow in the south through Derby to Brassington near Wirksworth. Beyond Brassington the old Roman road to Buxton was used. As was common with early turnpikes, this route merely improved the old roads, which were little better than packhorse trails and contained many steep gradients. In time this early turnpike road went out of use as routes with easier gradients were opened from Derby to Manchester via Ashbourne, Leek and Macclesfield.

As faster journey times for coaches and carriages were demanded, the emphasis shifted to providing easier gradients, and the old routes were either abandoned or modified. There was also a need to link the growing industrial towns – frequently in valleys near rivers – which had often been ignored by the old ridgeways. The next important route to be developed was the 1756 turnpike from Derby to Sheffield via Duffield, Holbrook and Chesterfield. Three years later the Nottingham to Newhaven turnpike was set up, which went via Alfreton, Oakerthorpe, Matlock, Winster and Pikehall. Today the section of this route through Snitterton seems incredible, given the narrowness of the lane, but it illustrates the need to avoid flood-prone riverside areas by climbing out of the Derwent Valley as fast as possible.

Toll cottage on Steep Turnpike, Matlock.

By the early nineteenth century road building had become more ambitious, as illustrated by the Cromford to Belper route, opened in 1820. This had originally gone uphill after Cromford Bridge to Castle Top, and then through Bow Wood, involving some steep gradients, but the later route ran alongside the Derwent as far as Lea Bridge, after stabilising work on the river banks. The old road network was often disrupted by the need to force travellers to use the new routes: near Winster the old Portway at the bottom of Dudwood Lane was blocked up in favour of the 1811 Ashbourne to Bakewell turnpike. As happened later with 'railway mania', some roads were constructed on the basis of wildly optimistic traffic forecasts; the 1818 road over the Snake Pass at 1,680 feet was designed by Telford to link Sheffield and Manchester. But by 1849 the trust was £107,000 in debt and the bulk of the traffic had shifted to the railways.

The turnpikes were still theoretically able to call on local labour for road repair, since statute labour was not abolished until the 1835 Highways Act. But in practice an Act of Parliament of 1776 allowed payment in lieu of work, and this income was given to the trusts via the parishes. Two Scottish engineers, Thomas Telford and John McAdam, introduced a more scientific approach to road construction, and the latter was especially influential in promoting a hardwearing and relatively cheap road surface. He emphasised the importance of using evenly sized stones, as well as providing proper drainage through culverts. A more local engineer was 'Blind Jack' of Naresborough, who was responsible for many roads in South Yorkshire and North Derbyshire.

The Cromford to Belper turnpike offers a good example of the operation of a later trust. Promoted by local industrialists such as the Strutts, Hurts and Arkwrights, who also became trustees, the focus was mainly on moving goods to and from the Derwent Valley's mills. The total length was eight miles, with a one-mile spur to Bullbridge. Opened in 1820, the route thrived until the late 1840s. In 1844, for instance, the trust received £1,168 in tolls, plus a further £194 in highway rates from local authorities. However, £360 was spent on labourers' wages, £228 on materials, and there was a debt of £21,000 to be serviced at 5% interest. This meant that the debt was actually increasing, even with quite a healthy income.

However, three years later in 1850, toll income dropped to £587, a fall of more than 50% on 1847. This was due to the opening of the Derby–Rowsley railway in 1849. A previous railway from Derby to Rotherham, the North Midland, had opened in 1840 with a station at Ambergate, but this hadn't appeared to affect the turnpike tolls. By 1873 income had dropped to £426, although there was also a decline in expenditure, with labour costs of only £200, and just £69 spent on materials. However, debts had been reduced to only £5,000, at 2.5% interest. Under an agreement of 1846 the railway company had paid a substantial sum (£7,200) for the trust to drop its opposition to the new line, and this must have contributed to the reduction in debt. It is curious that it was the rival railway that allowed the turnpike to clear most of its debts, before being wound up in 1887.

Today the workings of the turnpike trusts are largely forgotten, but they have left a clear legacy in the form of the routes that were developed at the time, such as the Snake Pass. A fair number of toll keepers' cottages have also survived, often extended and modernised, but recognisable by their closeness to the road. In addition, on some of the routes, such as Alfreton to Ashbourne, many of the milestones remain, while in places such as Crich market place horse drinking troughs can still be seen.

THE EFFECT OF ENCLOSURES

While it has been shown that some early enclosures date from pre-Conquest times,[27] and in fact enclosures occurred throughout the medieval period, depending on local conditions, it was the enclosures of the eighteenth and nineteenth centuries which most affected the modern road system.

An example of this can be seen by examining the high ground east of Tansley, Dethick and Lea on Burdett's map. In the 1760s

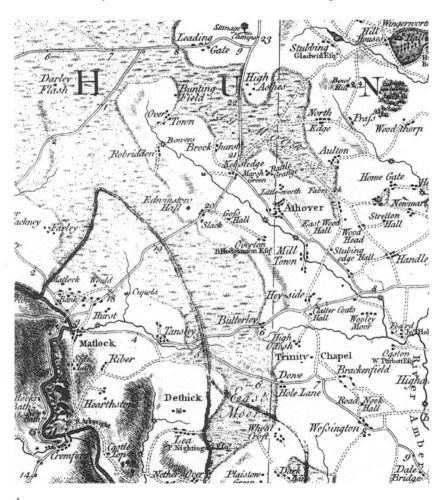

Burdett's map of East Moor, 1767.

this was still part of East Moor, which stretched almost as far south as Wakebridge. No doubt this moorland provided villagers with rough grazing and a supply of firewood. We know that there were packhorse tracks across the moor because of the guide stoop[28] on the Matlock–Brackenfield (A615) road, which indicates the direction of Wirksworth, Chesterfield, Bakewell and Derby, but these tracks are not shown on Burdett's map.

This area of moor was the subject of the Dethick, Lea and Holloway Enclosure Award[29] of 1777. This specified not only the course of the new roads needed to serve the enclosed fields, but also the width of the roads, the names of the roads, and the arrangements for their maintenance:

> *One other private carriage road and public drift road or way beginning at Upper Holloway and extending in a North Easterly direction over the said High Moor to the said Lea Road and from thence along the said Lea Road and High Street Road to the Southwardly corner of the allotment No. 17 and branching out from the said High Street Road and extending in a North Easterly direction to the Nottingham Turnpike road at Doehole Lane … which said road we have staked out to the breadth of 27 feet between the fences and we do hereby call the same Doehole Lane Road and we do order and direct that the same shall at all times for ever hereafter be repaired and kept in repair in such manner as other public highways and roads are by law directed to be repaired.*

The results of this award can be seen on Sanderson's map of 1835, which shows the new roads and fields. Note that at this date there was still one small unenclosed area, marked as The Common, on the Tansley–Brackenfield road.

In general, it was the highest and least profitable land that was enclosed the latest, since this would require the most investment to improve. Therefore, 'enclosure roads', which tend to be straight and of standard width, are most often found in the upland areas of Derbyshire, which were mainly enclosed in the late eighteenth or early nineteenth centuries.

Sanderson's map of Lea Moor, 1835.

COACHES AND WAGGONS

As in earlier times, prosperous and fairly healthy people preferred to travel on horseback in this period, which was generally seen as faster and more convenient: horses could be hired at many inns for those who didn't keep their own. Private coaches came into use in Elizabethan times, but initially their use was mainly confined to London streets. A century later public stagecoaches arrived, which completed long journeys in a series of stages, with overnight stops at coaching inns. These early coaches were slow, so that the journey from Derby to London could take five days: partly because of the state of the roads, but also due to their crude design.

Unsurprisingly, coach travel was unpopular as well as expensive, since people disliked being squeezed together for such lengthy journeys. Added to which they often involved very early starts, hurried meals *en route*, and late arrivals. As late as 1760 the 'Flying Machine' from Manchester to London, via Buxton and Derby, set off at four in the morning and arrived in London three days later at six in the evening: this was quite fast by the standards of previous decades. Only those unable or unwilling to ride used the stagecoaches, although they did provide some shelter in bad weather, at least for the six inside passengers. (There was room for more passengers on top or at the back, at a reduced price.)

Apart from smoother roads and gentler gradients, a significant improvement to travel was the introduction of steel springs on stagecoaches in about 1750. These meant it was possible to accomplish the journey from Manchester to London in just 18 hours by the early nineteenth century, avoiding the need for an overnight stop. Nevertheless, given the small number of passengers a coach could carry, fares remained high: in 1760 a journey from Derby to London cost £1-8-0 (one pound and eight shillings), the equivalent of about £260 today.

The Red Lion Inn, Wirksworth.

The rapid growth of stagecoach traffic meant an increasing demand for meals and overnight accommodation on the road. Old inns expanded and new ones were built at major intersections, for example the Peacock Inn at Oakerthorpe, or the New Inn at Newhaven. Most towns still have a recognisable coaching inn, such as the Red Lion at Wirksworth and the Rutland Arms in Bakewell, often with an arched entrance into a yard which would have contained stables. It was necessary to change horses every 12 miles or so in order to maintain speed, so that a sizeable horse economy grew up, comprising ostlers, farriers, coachmen, guards and all the indoor staff of the inns. It is estimated that in the heyday of coaching, in the 1830s, over 3,000 coaches were in use nationwide, needing 150,000 horses to operate.[30]

The reception given to travellers at inns was the subject of frequent friction, involving that essential English trait – snobbery. Those on horseback or in private coaches were the most welcome, and they could expect to eat in a private room, so as to avoid contact with the *hoi polloi*. Less welcome were stagecoach passengers, who complained that they were frequently kept waiting, or given food they didn't have time to eat, due to the rigorous timekeeping of the coaches. Their standard meal was called an 'ordinary', and was a set menu costing about 6d (sixpence). At the bottom of the pile were pedestrians and passengers in waggons, who were sometimes made to eat in the kitchen, or refused service altogether.

Stage waggons were the slowest and cheapest form of public transport available. They were large, clumsy-looking vehicles with wide wheels, often drawn by six horses. Unlike the coachmen, waggoners walked beside their team, while passengers shared the space with whatever goods had been entrusted to the carrier. An advert from the *Derby Mercury* for 1733 gives an idea of the speed of travel: 'George Paschall, now the old Derby carrier to London, sends a Waggon from his house adjoining to the Red Lyon Inn in Derby every Monday and is at the Bull and Mouth Inn near Aldersgate, London every Saturday'.[31]

They would certainly have been easy prey for robbers, and there was a report of a robbery of the Derbyshire waggon on Finchley Common in 1741, during which the waggoner was seriously injured by two knife-wielding 'footpads'. But stagecoaches were a potentially richer target for highwaymen, as shown by this report in the *Derby Mercury* in 1771: 'On Friday morning early the Derby coach was stopp'd near Kitts Inn, not far from St Albans by two highwaymen, who collected a considerable sum of money from the passengers, and wished them a good morning...'.[32]

Travellers who were robbed on the road had (theoretically) some claim for recompense from the parish they were travelling through, but this only applied from Monday to Saturday. Sunday travel was long considered disreputable, and is a cause of Fanny's disapproval of Henry Crawford in Jane Austen's novel *Mansfield Park*. Despite all these factors, the quantity of coach services and the number of travellers increased throughout the eighteenth century, so that there were regular services between Derby, Ashbourne, Lichfield, Matlock, Chesterfield, Sheffield and other large towns in the region.

Probably the best descriptions of road travel just before the coming of the railways can be found in Charles Dickens' *Pickwick Papers*, published in 1836. The unofficial hero, Samuel Weller, works as a 'boots' at the White Hart Inn in London, while his mother-in-law keeps the Marquis of Granby pub at Dorking, clearly Dickens' version of the ideal inn:

> *The Marquis of Granby in Mrs Weller's time was quite a model of a roadside public house of the better class – just large enough to be convenient and small enough to be snug... The bar window displayed a choice collection of geranium plants, and a well-dusted row of spirit phials. The open shutters bore a variety of golden descriptions, eulogistic of good beds and neat wines, and the choice group of countrymen and hostlers lounging about the stable-door and horse-trough, afforded presumptive proof of the excellent quality of the ale and spirits sold within.[33]*

WAYFARERS ALL

While the bulk of the British population was still essentially rural – which applied up until the 1840s – many people earned their living by serving the needs of country dwellers on their doorsteps. Higglers or swailers travelled from farm to farm buying eggs, cheese and whatever else was produced locally, in order to sell it on at market. Pedlars or packmen, however, carried lightweight goods from house to house, primarily to tempt the women in the household to buy cloth and personal items such as combs, brushes or similar. However, most of these itinerants have vanished from the historical record, having left little documentation except in diaries and stories at times. We can only guess at their numbers, or how ancient such occupations were, though it seems reasonable to assume that these services have a long history.

On 10 October 1800 Dorothy Wordsworth wrote:

> *The Cockermouth traveller came with thread, hardware, mustard etc. She is very healthy; has travelled over the mountains these thirty years. She does not mind the storms, if she can keep her goods dry. Her husband will not travel with an ass, because it is the tramper's badge; she would have one to relieve her from the weary load.*[34]

This short passage gives us an insight into the extraordinary (to us) ways people made ends meet at the time, as well as providing two other terms for pedlar. The name 'Cockermouth traveller' suggests that she had a regular route and presumably a repertoire of customers, remote from any shop, who were grateful for her visits. The Scots were often associated with this trade, as the name of a pub in Hathersage, called 'The Scotsman's Pack', suggests.

Pedlars, hawkers and hucksters appear to have been virtually synonymous, and David Hey[35] gives a useful account of what is known of their activities in the South Yorkshire and Derbyshire area. Since at least the Middle Ages itinerants of all types had been regarded with suspicion by the urban authorities, but in addition to the invariable

Noticeboard at Alport.

hostility to tramps and gypsies, pedlars and their ilk were seen as threatening the town shopkeepers' livings. Attempts were made from time to time to license pedlars, but by the nature of their work they were difficult to control. When a national register was set up in 1697, 2,500 individuals were listed, but only 19 of those were in Derbyshire – many more must have been operating unofficially. In 1851 the national census revealed over 25,000 pedlars, but this must also have been far from the true picture. As late as 1910, D.H. Lawrence's first novel, *The White Peacock*, portrays a Christmas scene:

> *… the carts of the hucksters dashed by to the expectant villagers, triumphant with great bunches of light foreign mistletoe, gay with oranges peeping through the boxes, and scarlet intrusion of apples, and wild confusion of cold, dead poultry.*[36]

The same concerns to regulate and authorise applied to the group of traders called badgers, swailers or higglers. Their role was essentially to buy produce where there was a surplus and to sell it where there was demand. For example, corn could be grown in the south and east of Derbyshire, but the cooler and damper northwest produced more dairy produce. The name badger or higgler suggests someone with a reputation for striking a hard bargain at the farm gate, but they provided an essential service, and Hey demonstrates how numerous they were: 179 licences were issued in 1748 at the Derbyshire Quarter Sessions, the majority for dealers from the northern half of the county. Presumably there were also others operating without a licence, and it is likely that this was frequently a part-time role for which the only requirements would be the use of a horse and panniers.

The 1841 census taken in Winster in June records the following:[37]

> *Slept on the turnpike roadside, in a tent, Richard Bryon, 30, Pot Carrier, Catherine Bryon, 25, Richard Bryon, 5, Emma Bryon, 3.*

This family may have been *en route* to a new home or they might have been regularly on the move: having a tent suggests the latter. The tramp, on the other hand, was a regular feature of rural life and folklore up to the mid-twentieth century. The very poorest members of society were forced to go begging from place to place, sleeping in barns, under hedges or, as George Orwell described in some detail,[38] in rural workhouses.

The tramp in Lawrence's early story 'Love Among the Haystacks' is portrayed in a way that reveals the author's respectable working-class prejudices:

> *A tramp was slouching towards them through the gap. He was a very seedy, slinking fellow, with a tang of horsey braggadocio about him. Small, thin and ferrety, with a week's red beard bristling on his pointed chin, he came slouching towards them.*[39]

But Dorothy Wordsworth was more sympathetic:

> *On Tuesday May 22nd a very tall woman … called at the door. She had on a very long brown cloak, and a very white cap, without bonnet; her face was excessively brown, but it had plainly once been fair. She led a little bare-footed child about two years old by the hand, and said her husband, who was a tinker, was gone before with the other children. I gave her a piece of bread.*[40]

Clearly there must have been many thousands of people like this on the road before the twentieth century, forced to travel in all weathers and dependent on the charity of strangers for their survival. At the other extreme were the drovers, jaggers, packmen and badgers who were respectable, licensed traders performing vital services. But in between there must have been others, such as the woman's tinker husband, who had a nominal trade but might well resort to begging when times were hard.

6

The Eighteenth Century: Drovers, tourists, the minister and the farmer

DROVE ROADS

With the growth of major industrial cities in the eighteenth century, demand for fresh meat meant an increase in long-distance droving, especially from Wales and Scotland. But little of this traffic passed through the Peak District, and most herding of animals would have been to and from local livestock markets. Dodd and Dodd[41] suggest one possible droving route from Hartington through Newhaven, Cardlemere Lane, Minninglow Lane, Summer Lane near Wirksworth, Alport Height, Ambergate, Bullbridge and on to Nottingham. Drovers, who needed to be licensed and were generally well-respected men responsible for hundreds of pounds' worth of stock, would have

Possible drove road near Minninglow.

preferred to avoid paying tolls on turnpikes. In addition, they would need to find grazing for the animals *en route*, either by the roadside or in rented pastures when they stopped for the night.

There is a lack of documentary evidence on this topic: few drovers' records survive and none appear to have written about their lives. Yet the sight of herds of cows or flocks of sheep on the road to the nearest market or fair were familiar up to the early twentieth century; many farmers, whether buying or selling, would have had little alternative. It may be possible to identify a few examples of 'drove roads', as mentioned above, by their unusual width, but most herding would be along ordinary roads.

Drovers must have used the same roads several times a year, so presumably they had little need for navigation aids, but from the late seventeenth century some provision was made for helping other travellers. The first practical road maps were the strip maps surveyed by John Ogilby and published in 1675.[42] They simply focus on the course of the main roads, showing junctions, villages, hills and other useful features. However, only one of the 100 maps published in Ogilby's *Britannia*, showing the Derby–Manchester road, covers the area north of Derby.

Guidestoop near junction of Bonsall Lane above Winster, giving directions of Leek, Wirksworth, Bonsall and Bakewell.

Probably more useful than these maps were the guide stoops installed by parishes after 1709, on the instruction of local magistrates. These had initially been ordered by an Act of 1697, and were intended to give the direction of the nearest market towns at crossroads in moorland areas, where travellers were unlikely to find local help. Forty-six of these stone pillars remain in Derbyshire, though many have been moved from their original position, and a few have been recycled as gateposts. Despite this, they provide a useful indicator to routes in the pre-turnpike era, and may even show where a road has been lost (see Chapter 8F). Howard Smith's comprehensive study of the subject has full details of all surviving stoops.[43]

EARLY TOURISTS

It is interesting to compare the reports of the first tourists to Derbyshire in the eighteenth century with the records left by some of the county's inhabitants. The idea of travelling for pleasure seems to have developed in the late seventeenth century, as stability and peace were established after the accession of William and Mary to the throne. This was also the period when taking the waters at newly developed spas such as Bath, Tunbridge Wells, and locally Buxton and Matlock became fashionable. Celia Fiennes was an enterprising female traveller who toured the Peak District on horseback, with a couple of servants, in 1697. This is her description of the journey from Bakewell to Buxton:

> *Its very difficult to find the Wayes here for you see only tops of hills and so many roads – by reason of ye best wayes up and down – that its impossible for Coach or Waggon to pass some of y^m , and you scarce see a tree and No hedges all over ye Country, only dry stone walls y^t incloses ground no other ffence. Buxton we Saw 2 or 3 tymes and then Lost ye sight of it as often, and at last did not See it till just you Came upon it – that 9 mile we were above 6 hours going it. The house thats Call'd Buxton Hall wch belongs to ye Duke of Devonshire its where the warme bath is and well, its the Largest house in the place tho› not very good; they are all Entertaining houses and its by way of an ordinary – so much a piece for ye dinners and suppers and so much for our Servants besides; all ye ale and wine is to be paid–besides, the beer they allow at the meales is so bad y^t very Little Can be dranke. You pay not for ye bed roome and truely the other is so unreasonable a price and ye Lodgings so bad, 2 beds in a Roome some 3 beds and 4 in one roome, so that if you have not Company Enough of your own to fill a Room they will be ready to put others into the same Chamber, and sometymes they are so Crowded that three must Lye in a bed. Few people stay above two or three nights its so Inconvenient.[44]*

In dramatizing the steepness of the gradients and the barrenness of the landscape Fiennes strikes a Romantic note which will be echoed throughout the period, and her experience of staying at Buxton is a reminder of the lack of privacy which was common at the time.

Daniel Defoe visited the county in 1726, when he experienced the difficulties of travelling in a rainy period. Clearly, less than 300 years ago the state of the rivers could be highly disruptive:

*So from Derby we went to Dove-Bridge, or as the country people call it,
Dowbridge, where we had the pleasure to see the river drowning the low-
grounds by a sudden shower, and hastning to the Trent with a most outrageous
stream, in which there being no great diversion, and travelling being not very
safe in a rainy season on that side, we omitted seeing Ashbourn and Uttoxeter
.... two market towns upon that river, and returning towards Derby, we
went from thence directly up into the High Peak. Hence we kept the Derwent
on our right-hand, but kept our distance, the waters being out; for the Derwent
is a frightful creature when the hills load her current with water.*[45]

Near the end of the century, in 1790, Lord Torrington was unhappy
with his reception in Bakewell:

*I was never in a nastier house [The Rutland Arms]. I often arose from my
very bad bed to look at the weather, very rainy, a gloomy black morning,
all the hills covered by thick mists .... Master or Mistress not to be seen
probably having been drunk overnight.*[46]

DERBYSHIRE DIARISTS

Compared with these visitors, the diaries of James Clegg, a dissenting
minister at Chapel-en-le-Frith, and Mathew Gibbons, a Rowsley
farmer, give us an indication of the movements of fairly ordinary
Derbyshire people in the eighteenth century. Clegg came from
Lancashire but was invited to lead the congregation at Malcoff, in north
Derbyshire, in 1703. Meetings were held in Chinley Chapel, Chapel
Milton, near Chapel-en-le-Frith, an area with strong Presbyterian
sympathies. James married Ann Campion from Edale in 1704 and
eventually leased a farm near Chapel-en-le-Frith called Stoddart Hall.
In addition to farming and preaching he also became a doctor, and was
often called to visit the sick in distant hamlets.[47]

Chinley Chapel, near Chapel-en-le-Frith.

Chinley Chapel still functions, a well-cared-for building in a tranquil graveyard, though it is now overshadowed by massive stone railway viaducts, making it hard to imagine the scene here in the early eighteenth century. Clegg probably walked the area around his home village, where he had frequent business concerns, but rode his mare for longer journeys, which were made at all seasons and in all weathers. His diary occasionally records some of the hazards and discomforts of travel before the turnpike era, but clearly this did not prevent him from making frequent and lengthy journeys.

An analysis of the significant journeys Clegg made in the first six months of 1730 (Appendix 3), presumably on horseback and at the age of 51, reveals that he rode nearly a thousand miles. The figures are only approximate, as it is impossible to know his exact routes, but these journeys illustrate the network of interests, family, friends and community responsibilities which Clegg maintained, and which were probably typical of someone in his position. It is notable that journey lengths increase with better weather and longer days, from 69 miles in January to 286 in May.

During this half year he made four visits to Manchester, where a son lived, and two trips to the Chesterfield area, where his sister lived at Calow. Macclesfield, Derby, Ashford and Stanton were also included in his travels. The maximum journey in one day seems to have been just under 30 miles, which is probably the greatest distance his horse could manage. Four mph is considered a good speed for a horse and rider over a long distance, so the journey to Chesterfield could have taken over seven hours.

Mathew Gibbons was a young farmer in Rowsley who kept a diary[48] for the two years 1761 and 1762, recording the farming tasks done by his family and the movements of his father, mother and himself. This shows that during these two years they visited at least 18 towns and villages in the county, as shown in Appendix 4.

As might be expected, nearby places such as Beeley and Darley were visited most often, but quite lengthy journeys to Chesterfield and even Derby were also made in these years. The reasons for the journeys were mainly attending church services and farm business. Mathew, who was 19 when he started diary-keeping, seems to have been fond of going to church as he often attended two services on Sundays, frequently at Beeley and often at Darley or Bakewell too. The family observed the Sabbath quite strictly (no record of farm work on Sundays) and also kept many of the old Saints' Days (e.g. All Saints: 1 November) as holidays.

Farm business could involve delivering loads (e.g. thatch) by cart, or buying and selling livestock at a fair, such as at Matlock or Bakewell. Some of the journeys to Derby and Chesterfield were to buy seeds, but Mathew also often went with his mother to Bakewell market on Mondays, perhaps for more domestic shopping. Trips to feasts, wakes, burials and similar may have had a social element, as well as being

The old road from Rowsley to Bakewell, which Mathew Gibbons would have used.

an opportunity for shopping. Drinking seems to have been a crucial part of the men's lives, with many references to getting drunk.

The Bakewell–Chesterfield turnpike was only authorised in 1760, so it is unlikely that it was in use at this date. The road into Matlock was a turnpike, although it followed a different course to the modern A6. But the diary gives no clues as to the form of travel or the condition of the roads. Presumably Gibbons rode to most places, though he would probably have taken his mother to Bakewell by cart. Another interesting sidelight is provided by the record of the statutory labour that Mathew and his father were required to perform on local roads for six days of the year.

How typical was this family of country people in the mid-eighteenth century? It is difficult to say, and the act of keeping a diary is itself unusual. However, the farming activities must have been fairly standard, and in other respects the family's behaviour appears quite traditional. The records of Clegg and Gibbons certainly suggest that people in the early modern period were more mobile than is often supposed. Both of them travelled around the district for a variety of reasons: to visit relatives, to attend religious services and to help friends and neighbours, as well as on purely business-related journeys, such as attending markets.

Given the lack of earlier records, it is interesting to speculate how far back in time this pattern of journeying might have extended.

Would a yeoman in the late medieval period have behaved in the same way? The technology of travel in 1760 had changed little since, say, 1460. Clearly, the state of the roads was not so bad as to prevent non-essential travel, and it was taken for granted by locals, if not by visitors. However, some of Clegg's accounts of riding on winter nights ('the night being very dark I narrowly escaped a dangerous fall into a stone pitt which my mare jumped into')[49] are a reminder of how rough conditions could have been, and of the exposure to wind and rain that riders had to endure all year round.

_7_

On the Move in the Nineteenth Century

A TASTE FOR GOTHIC

While the earliest tourists to Derbyshire such as Celia Fiennes and Daniel Defoe felt threatened by the wildness of the district and its rivers, later in the eighteenth century the same scenery became valued for its romantic drama. Inspired by contemporary poets such as Wordsworth and painters like Turner, fashionable folk had come to value rocky ravines and brooding moorland. The Derby artist Joseph Wright had earlier dramatised the scenery with his moonlight views, and also depicted the new industrial sites, such as Richard Arkwright's mill lit up at night.

One early set of attractions were the Seven Wonders of the Peak. These were first described in the seventeenth century and included a variety of wonderful and not-so-wonderful sites, among them the Peak Cavern at Castleton and the ebbing and flowing well at Tideswell.[50] Elizabeth Bennett, heroine of Jane Austen's *Pride and Prejudice*, goes on a tour of Derbyshire with her aunt and uncle, travelling by chaise to view 'all the celebrated beauties of Matlock, Chatsworth, Dovedale or the Peak'.[51] But as the nineteenth century began, visitors were equally interested in seeing the mills and factories that had sprung up along the River Derwent, and Arkwright built what is now the Greyhound Hotel in Cromford to accommodate some of them.

Painting of High Tor, Matlock, in the nineteenth century. Artist unknown.

SPAS AND HYDROS

Improved turnpike roads and better sprung coaches and chaises must have played their part in the popularisation of the area, as did the long Napoleonic Wars which prevented Continental travel until 1815. The horrors of nature could now be viewed in more comfort, and the quality of accommodation improved as well. Buxton had been an attraction for centuries, but it was both remote and chilly, at an altitude of about 1,000 feet. Matlock Bath had a suitably dramatic setting below High Tor and was more easily reached from the south. Access was improved in about 1815 by cutting through the rock at Scarthin Nick, by Cromford, which replaced the difficult old route over the Scarthin Rock. Earlier, in 1791, Anthony Gell of Hopton had improved the valley route from Cromford to the northwest by building the Via Gellia.

By 1800 the Old Bath, the New Bath and the Temple Hotels provided accommodation for hundreds of visitors to Matlock. Whereas Defoe had complained that 'This bath would be much more frequented than it is, if two things did not hinder; namely, a base, stony, mountainous road to it, and no good accommodation when you are there';[52] before the end of the eighteenth century Lipscomb could claim 'it has gaiety without dissipation, activity without noise, and facility of communication with other parts of the country undisturbed by the bustle of a public road'.[53] Visitors were offered strolls in Lovers' Walk below the Tor, trips to Chatsworth and Haddon Hall, and visits to the mills at Cromford. A full account of the development of tourism in the region is given in *The Discovery of the Peak District* by Trevor Brighton.[54]

In the early part of D.H. Lawrence's *The Rainbow*, which is set in the 1870s, the farmer Tom Brangwen rides from Cossall to Matlock:

> *One Whitsuntide he went a jaunt with two other young fellows, on horseback, to Matlock and thence to Bakewell. Matlock was at that time*

just becoming a famous beauty-spot, visited from Manchester and from the Staffordshire towns. In the hotel where the young men took lunch, were two girls, and the parties struck up a friendship.[55]

In fact, by this time the spa of Matlock Bath, which lies between Cromford and Matlock, was acquiring a rather racy reputation, partly as a result of the coming of the railway in 1849 and the consequent hike in visitor numbers. Nonetheless Buxton, its larger and older rival, maintained its popularity with some, as shown in Arnold Bennett's *The Old Wives' Tale*, which has Constance and Samuel Povey honeymooning there, again in a mid-nineteenth century setting.[56]

It seems likely that there is a link between the pre-Reformation tradition of pilgrimage, which often involved visiting a holy well, such as St Ann's at Buxton, the eighteenth-century enthusiasm for taking

Swiss chalet-style railway station at Matlock Bath, date uncertain.

the waters at a spa, and the nineteenth-century fashion for a cure at a hydro, such as sprang up at Matlock Bank (in Matlock itself) after 1850. St Ann's well was suppressed by Henry VIII's Protestant zealots in 1538, but the same concern for a health cure led to the growth of spas two hundred years later, while the hydro movement can be seen as a more (apparently) scientific treatment involving some of the same elements: water and a change of scene.

John Smedley, a mill owner at Lea Bridge, was responsible for developing Matlock Bank as a major centre for hydrotherapy from the mid-nineteenth century. He did not invent the treatment, but his establishment (now the offices of Derbyshire County Council) was constructed on an impressive scale and attracted thousands of patients annually, along with the dozen or so other smaller hydros that followed his lead. Most of the patients would arrive by rail, but their presence helped to stimulate the business of tourism in the area: the petrifying wells and caverns, the pleasure gardens and the gift shops which have continued to attract visitors ever since.

THE CLARION CALL

For those lower down the social scale, spas and hydros were probably out of reach, but by the 1880s the mill hands and factory girls of nearby cities, especially Sheffield and Manchester, were beginning to make their way into Derbyshire to escape, if only for a day, the smoke and grime of those places. By this time the bicycle had developed into a reasonably safe and affordable machine: its design now included two wheels of equal size, the rear one driven by a chain, and pneumatic tyres were also coming into use. Although the roads were still quite rough, and punctures must have been common, personal mobility was available to ordinary people for the first time. However, as a new bike would still cost about £12 in the 1890s, ownership was nonetheless limited to the more prosperous among the working class, since this price represented over a month's wages for a skilled workman. The growth of cycling was especially important for women's emancipation, since despite the inevitable cries of horror which first greeted female cyclists, these pioneers soon demonstrated that riding a bicycle was a healthy and enjoyable activity for both sexes.

By the 1890s cyclists were setting up clubs, notably the Clarion Cycling Club (which still exists). This was an offshoot of the Clarion movement, a socialist organisation based in the Midlands and the north of England, which was originally inspired by Robert Blatchford's influential weekly newspaper *The Clarion*. The Club held its first national meeting at Ashbourne in 1895, and thereafter combined the pleasures of the open road with distributing left-wing leaflets. Although men seem to have predominated in the clubs, early photos show a sprinkling of women among them.

At this time and on into the twentieth century there was a link between cyclists, walkers, climbers, and 'progressive' social movements, based either in chapels or co-operative societies. For the first time working-class people had the leisure to be tourists, albeit on a local and limited scale. This is well-illustrated by the walk described by Lawrence in *Sons and Lovers*, based on a real walk done at Easter 1905. A mixed group of young people, family and friends – mainly members of the Eastwood Congregational Church – walked from Alfreton to Ambergate via Wingfield Manor, which was the focus of the outing:

> *The manor is of hard, pale grey stone, and the outer walls are blank and calm. The young folk were in raptures. They went in trepidation, almost afraid that the delight of exploring this ruin might be denied them. .... All eagerly paid their sixpences, and went timidly through the fine clean arch of the inner courtyards. They were shy.*[57]

Walking in the countryside was first popularised by the Romantic poets at the turn of the nineteenth century. William Wordsworth and Samuel Taylor Coleridge both undertook walking tours which were later memorialised in poems such as *Lines Written a Few Miles above Tintern Abbey* (Wordsworth, 1798). Many similar books and poems followed, such as George Borrow's *Wild Wales* (1862) and Robert Louis Stevenson's *Travels with a Donkey* (1879).

One of the earliest walking clubs was The Manchester Association for the Preservation of Ancient Public Footpaths, established in 1826. The Manchester area remained vigorous in promoting walkers' rights,

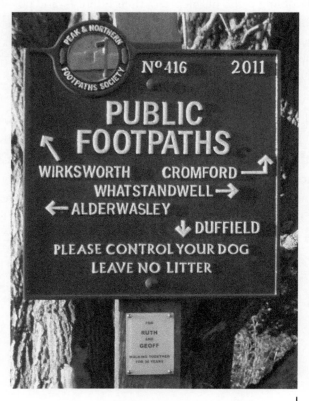

Peak and Northern footpath sign No. 416

and in 1894 The Peak District and Northern Counties Footpath Preservation Association was formed,[58] covering Derbyshire, Cheshire and Staffordshire as well as Lancashire and parts of Yorkshire. Although the Association's first focus was around access to the Kinder Scout moors, today its distinctive steel signs aid walkers throughout the region.

The Derbyshire Archaeological and Natural History Society,[59] founded in 1878, was typical of the many county societies which sprang up at this time, with an interest in field trips and botany as well as history. These bodies were more middle-class and scholarly than the rambling clubs, but in places their interests, and possibly their membership, overlapped.

A concern with defending rights of way seems to be an integral part of English culture. Many towns and villages remember instances of battles with high-handed landowners, such as Bakewell Council's struggles with the Marquess of Granby over paths around Haddon Hall in the 1920s.[60] The ramblers and hikers who first took to the paths of Derbyshire in the late nineteenth century have helped preserve this invaluable legacy of public rights of way, which in many places trace the tracks used by pilgrims and packhorses, higglers and highwaymen, Romans and Saxons, drovers and swalers down through the years. These routes comprise a heritage virtually unique to England; a heritage which today's walkers can appreciate, maintain and enjoy.

8

Walking the Portway

INTRODUCTION

This chapter explores the Portway as a route for the modern walker, broken up into eight stages. The various stages can be walked independently and in some cases can be included in a circular walk. The walk is described from south to north, i.e. from Nottingham to the Woodlands Valley. It is of course perfectly possible to walk the route in the opposite direction!

Each section provides a detailed historical overview and discussion of the points of interest along that part of the route. There is a map of the route to follow, and the section concludes with a box offering some practical information for finding the path on the ground.

Note that all the maps are diagrammatic and not to scale. They are included for orientation, but walkers are advised to use the OS 1:25,000 or 1:50,000 maps (Ordnance Survey Landranger sheets

129, 128, 119 and 110) for more detailed information, and to carry a compass. Most of the route is easy walking, although suitable footwear and clothing is clearly advisable.

Appendix 5 provides an overview of the Portway route and related historical sites along the way.

THE PORTWAY IN EIGHT STAGES

    A. Sneinton to the Hemlock Stone

    B. The Hemlock Stone to Dale

    C. Dale to Coxbench

    D. Coxbench to Alport Height

    E. Alport Height to Winster

    F. Winster to Ashford-in-the-Water

    G. Ashford-in-the-Water to Mam Tor

    H. Edale and the Woodlands Valley

A. SNEINTON TO THE HEMLOCK STONE

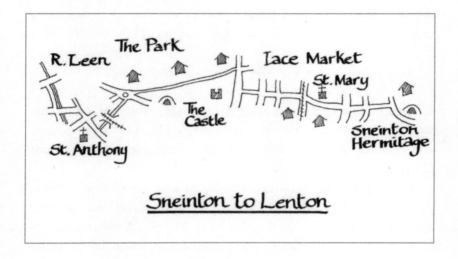

Tracing the route of an ancient trackway through a modern city might appear a Quixotic task. Layer upon layer of development must have obliterated all trace of what might have been, two thousand years or more ago. But my search was based on two presumptions. Firstly, that once established, roads in built-up areas have a habit of staying put, especially where they become edged by buildings. Secondly, the noted preference for travelling on higher ground, which in this case would mean keeping clear of the Trent floodplain and climbing over the rock that Nottingham was first built on, and then using the ridge now called the Bramcote Hills.

Assuming that the Portway was a route from the Trent through Derbyshire and over the Pennines, then it probably began at the riverside downstream of the modern Trent Bridge, where a bridge was built as early as 924 CE. The river has certainly shifted its course on the floodplain over the centuries, so the most convenient starting point for this walk seems to be Sneinton Hermitage, a group of caves in the sandstone rock below what was Sneinton village, to the east of Nottingham. Nineteenth-century engravings show a more extensive cluster of caves than exist today, many of which were destroyed by railway development, but the name goes back to at least 1501:

> *The Ermytage in Sneynton, being a house cutte out of the rocke.*[51]

As there are four hermitages along the Portway, it is worth stating that hermitages were often established in lonely places by religious men who wanted solitude, but who nevertheless needed to eat, and so made a living by guiding travellers.

Nottingham was frequently painted looking west from Sneinton Hill in the seventeenth and eighteenth centuries, and these pictures show a road running from there up to St Mary's Church, which was then on the eastern edge of the town's development. In the valley between the two settlements was a stream called The Beck, which ran

Sneinton Hermitage, Nottingham.

down into the River Leen just below the Hermitage. The crossing of this brook must have been the subject of a presentment of 1579:

> *Wee presente the cawse [causeway] a gaynste Snenton Forth [Ford] to be graveled, for when waters be owt, hit is so deepe worne that hitt dothe ovarthrow packe horses.*[62]

The reference to packhorses suggests that this was a long-distance route at the time, not merely a local track to Nottingham Market. Paul Sandby's 1750 engraving shows a footbridge over the stream at a spot called 'Penny-foot Stile', presumably the site of today's Pennyfoot Street. This leads into Fisher Gate and then climbs steeply up the rock, either by Hollow Stone or possibly the narrow pedestrian Malin Gate. These streets join at St Mary's Church in the centre of what was the original Saxon settlement and which later became the Lace Market. St Mary's has been the principal church and centre of civic life here for over a thousand years, and the present building is at least the third one on the site.

Jan Siberechts: 'View of Nottingham from the east' c.1700.

From here the road is called High Pavement, and leads past the old law courts to Weekday Cross, near which the trams now rumble down to the station. The cross, which is a modern replacement of older versions, marks the site of the original town market, held before the larger, lower market-place was developed after the Norman Conquest. The route now continues downhill as Low Pavement, then crosses Lister Gate and becomes Castle Gate. This leads up to the Royal Children Inn, which is one of Nottingham's oldest pubs, although the current building only dates from the 1930s. After crossing the modern Maid Marian Way, the route then continues up to the castle gate-house. This is one of the few surviving parts of the medieval castle,[63] and it is the source of endless disappointment to visitors who, having watched films about Robin Hood, expect to find a real story-book castle on the site.

After climbing up to the castle, the route now goes steadily downhill on Lenton Road through the privately-owned Park estate – an area of middle-class villas developed in the nineteenth century. This is the only road through the Park shown on George Sanderson's 1835 map, which reveals the estate as still largely undeveloped. The first part of Lenton Road appears to be cut into the sandstone, it then drops down to cross Peveril Drive before rising again.

On the left is Hermitage Walk, which no longer leads to any caves, since these have been closed off. But they are illustrated in an 1849 painting by W. Bradbury – *Druidical Remains, Nottingham Park* – which shows a pleasure ground with caves as a backdrop, and they are also marked on Sanderson's map by the same name (see map on p.11). The caves still exist but are now behind a gated housing complex on Castle Boulevard. One of the caves is a rock-hewn chapel, originally called St Mary de la Roche. This is thought to have been created by Carmelite Friars in the late thirteenth century and to have housed a shrine for a holy relic – again suggesting that this is on the line of a pilgrimage route. Later the chapel became connected to Lenton Priory, less than a mile away.[64]

Hermitage Walk, The Park, Nottingham.

The next part of Lenton Road becomes Park Road, and it finishes at a roundabout by the now-derelict Grove pub. Abbey Bridge crosses the railway leading into Abbey Street, which is confusing, as the monastery here was generally known as a Priory. Following instead along Grove Road, a low-level pedestrian path leads to St Anthony's Church, which is virtually the only relic of Lenton Priory surviving today.[65]

The Priory was founded by William Peveril early in the twelfth century as a Cluniac house. Richly endowed with land, the church was considered similar in size to Southwell Minster, and the monastery continued to function for four hundred years until the Dissolution in 1538. It seems remarkable that such a huge structure could completely disappear, yet the ruins must have provided a useful quarry for local builders, including for the construction of nearby Wollaton Hall by Sir Francis Willoughby.

The history of the River Leen, which of course gave its name to Lenton, is quite complex in this area. A map of 1632[66] shows the site of the Priory enclosed in a tight bend of the river, which was diverted

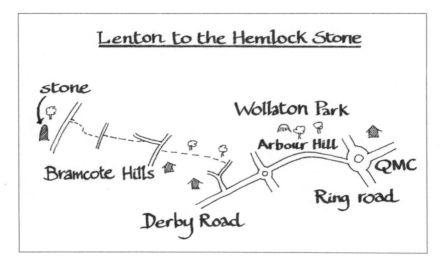

in the late eleventh century to run under the Castle rock, near to the course of the later Nottingham Canal. But a flood protection measure in the 1960s restored the main flow to its original north/south course, joining the Trent near Riverside Way.

Not only would the Priory have provided a focus for pilgrimage, but it was also the site of the Lenton Fair, held for eleven days at Martinmas in November. This was an important trading occasion, and markets in Nottingham were forbidden during fair days. Merchants and customers must have been attracted from a wide radius, and the Portway would have been used by many of them. Remarkably, the Fair continued to be held right up to the early twentieth century, although latterly it had become mainly a horse fair.[67]

From here the route is obscure for some distance. The simplest way is to cross Abbey Street by the White Hart pub and take Leen Gate to the hospital complex of the Queen's Medical Centre (QMC), turning right there to follow the canalised river up to Derby Road. Turn left in front of the Wollaton Hall lodge gates, which look incongruous in this setting, and follow Derby Road to the ring road. All the land to the north was bought by the City of Nottingham when the Wollaton Hall estate was sold in the 1920s, and some of the peripheral land was used for housing development.

A substantial brick wall still surrounds Wollaton Park, which is entered through a stone gateway called Beeston Lodge. Inside the Park, Arbour Hill can be seen and visited to the right, on the edge of the golf course. This may have been the first 'port' or defensive encampment on the route, and lies about four miles from Sneinton.

Beyond the next roundabout the route of the Portway diverges from Derby Road, taking to higher ground. Although this area was built up with suburban housing developments in the 1960s and 1970s, there is still a green spine running along the top of the ridge, which has been designated as part nature reserve and part park. It can be accessed from several streets, and paths run west towards Thoresby Road. One of these tracks is bordered by what seems an ancient hedge, suggesting that this way pre-dates all the modern development. On the far side of Thoresby Road is the defunct Bramcote Hill golf course, but this can be skirted by following Deddington Lane and further paths to reach Coventry Lane opposite the Bramcote Crematorium.

From here the Hemlock Stone is a short walk to the left, and can be found in a park clearing on the west side of the road. It is an impressive, heavily weathered sandstone column, standing over six metres high. Although there are outcrops of sandstone all around Nottingham, this is quite different in terms of size and prominence. The bottom is reddish, but the top half is darker. There is no indication that it is anything but a natural feature yet, given the softness of the sandstone, it could have been cut or modified by human activity to create a marker.

Over the years there has been much inconclusive speculation about both the name and history of this stone. There are associations with the spring festival of Beltane, which was marked by the lighting

The Hemlock Stone, Bramcote.

of bonfires. According to Ronald Hutton,[68] the hill is one of the few places in England with documented evidence of the celebration of such May Day (or Beltane) festivities. The stone could have acted as a route marker on the southern section of the Portway, given that it would be visible to travellers coming from the west towards the Erewash crossing a mile away. There is also the possibility that it was a boundary marker to advise travellers that they were entering a new tribal territory, 'hem' meaning edge or border. The Hemlock Stone also features in D.H. Lawrence's *Sons and Lovers*, where it was the focus of another Easter walk from Eastwood (which also took place in 1905). Lawrence describes the Bank Holiday scene: 'Everywhere in the field below, factory girls and lads were eating lunch or sporting about.'[69]

WALKING: SNEINTON TO THE HEMLOCK STONE (ABOUT 7 MILES)

*S*neinton Hermitage is easily reached from Nottingham Midland Station. Follow Station Street east to London Road, turn left and then cross the road and continue walking east past the BBC offices. This brings you to Manvers Street, and the Hermitage is found a little further on the left.

Directions from the Hermitage to Lenton will be found in the text above. Beyond Lenton, the route on Derby Road is uncomfortable walking due to the volume of traffic. The first section can be walked on the service road on the north side. After crossing the ring road, the service road can be followed up to the first entrance from the main road, but after this point there is no option but to walk beside the A52. However, this is worth doing for the chance to enter the Park at the lodge gate.

Beyond the Wollaton Vale roundabout, continue on Derby Road to David Grove, follow this to Heather Rise on the right, and a footpath sign can be seen which leads into the ridge park. Follow paths westward and you should eventually drop down onto Thoresby Road. Deddington Lane is a little to the right, and this shortly becomes a footpath that continues to the narrow Moor Lane. Almost opposite is another path which takes you to Coventry Lane, by the Plymouth Brethren's meeting room. Turn left here, with Bramcote Hills Park on both sides of the road, and the Hemlock Stone is on the right.

B. THE HEMLOCK STONE TO DALE

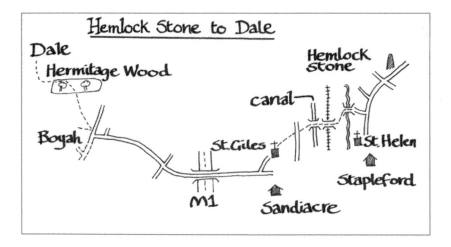

In establishing the line of the Portway at the boundary between Nottinghamshire and Derbyshire the crucial factor is the river crossing. Although the Erewash (the 'meandering stream') today is only a few yards wide, it must have been a much more serious obstacle before being confined within its present banks. The name Stapleford is Saxon, meaning 'ford marked by a post'.

The present church of St Helen dates from 1220 CE, but in the churchyard is a remarkable ancient cross, which might have been the post (or 'steeple') from which the town derives its name. It is the oldest church monument in the county, and has been dated by various sources to between 700 and 1100 CE, but most recently to about 920. Although now in the churchyard, it has had at least one other location, so it is unclear where it was originally sited. It is also noticeably un-cross-like, without arms, but covered in scrollwork and the upper part has four faces, much worn, with carvings of what may be an angel and a serpent. One of the figures might represent St Luke. It could well have served both as a base for travelling preachers and as a marker for the ford. Over the road the Old Cross pub reinforces the significance of the monument, which probably greatly predates any other structure in the town.

By the Erewash, the Old Mill is today a rundown-looking working men's club, but it may be the same building as the watermill shown at this site on Sanderson's 1835 map, with a millpond to the north, no trace of which is visible now. What is significant is the line of the footpath route, which runs from here over the river and the water meadows, then via a long ugly bridge over the railway line and sidings, before crossing the Erewash Canal. Clearly,

Stapleford Cross,
St Helen's churchyard, Stapleford.

this route was important enough to keep open when new modes of transport came along, suggesting long usage. From the canal bridge there is a spectacular westerly view of the church at Sandiacre, with Church Farm in front, high up on the Derbyshire side of the valley.

Standing in St Giles' churchyard at Sandiacre the spires of Stapleford and Bramcote are clearly visible, which would have given travellers along the west-east route a good idea of the next stage of the road. The church of St Giles is peculiar in many ways. Situated on the northern fringe of the modern town, which developed to the south around the old Derby Road, it is perched on a hilltop, with a Romanesque nave and a taller fourteenth-century chancel. Nikolaus Pevsner[70] describes it as 'the most interesting in the neighbourhood'.

Capital in St Giles Church, Sandiacre.

Its prominent siting may be explained by its position on the line of the Portway, serving as a landmark and possibly as a shrine for pilgrimage. The nave is possibly pre-Conquest, with a remarkable arch leading to the chancel, the capitals richly carved with bizarre figures.

Sandiacre is the first place on the route with a documentary reference to the 'Portweye'. R.W.P. Cockerton[71] tells us that the name occurs several times in a thirteenth-century charter of Dale Abbey, the road acting as a boundary to various pieces of land, some of which can still be identified in the vicinity of the route. On the Sanderson map Stanton Road is called Ladycroft Lane. However, one of the last houses on the right – before crossing the M1 motorway – which appears to date from the late-nineteenth century, was called Ladycross Cottage. It seems clear therefore that the road was actually called Lady*cross* Lane, which suggests a roadside cross in this vicinity, perhaps marking the route to St Mary's (Our Lady's) Abbey at Dale. The 1896 Ordnance Survey map also shows a large house near here named Ladycross House, and there is a Ladycross Infants School in the town.

The next stage of the route, after crossing the Risley Road, is called No Man's Lane, the meaning of which is unclear, though it may be an ironic reference to Ladycross Lane (i.e. lady = no man). An alternative suggestion by Cockerton[72] is that the road was not the responsibility of either bordering parish, so the name means 'unadopted'. It soon becomes obvious that this is a ridgeway with remarkable views, first over the Trent valley to the south, and then into the White Peak to the north. Crich Stand and Alport Height are visible on the horizon, as are Bramcote Hills and the Hemlock Stone looking back east, while the white sails of the Cat and Fiddle Windmill make a distinctive landmark to the northwest.

Where the road makes a sharp right turn, Boyah Grange lies straight in front, consisting of two large farmhouses set back from the road down a track. Cockerton[73] suggests that the original line of the Portway ran through Boyah. The field between the farmhouses and the road is full of bumps and hollows, often flooded, and is called the Cunnery on old maps, suggesting the keeping of rabbits, but this does not explain the origin of the earthworks which encouraged the animals to burrow there. 'Grange' means a monastic farm, which is not surprising with an abbey only a mile away. The farmhouse is a listed building, and it is possible that it was a moated site in the medieval period.

A Roman aisled hall was excavated between 1994 and 1997 a mile to the southwest at Hay Grange. The report[74] shows that this area was in mixed cultivation by the late Iron Age, before the Romans arrived, although the economic changes they brought about probably stimulated agricultural production. One interesting aspect of the dig was the large quantity of lead objects found; it appears that this metal was cheap at the time, possibly because the Romans were extracting silver from the lead ore and so needed to process large quantities, leading to a glut of lead.

The field path from Boyah to Dale is in alignment with the last part of No Man's Lane, and presumably the Portway would have dropped down into Dale on the grass slope between the two sections of rocky outcrop, to the west of the present footpath. The hermitage, cut into the cliff face, seems improbably open for year-round occupation, but possibly a wooden framework, let into the cliff face, would have given more protection and space. This is a lovely spot, with good views over the valley through the trees, which might have compensated for the drawbacks of cave life.

The legend of the foundation of Dale Abbey begins with the story of a devout Derby baker who was told by St Mary in a dream

All Saints Church, Dale. A rare semi-detached church.

to abandon his home and go to live in Depedale, at that time an unpopulated forest. It is claimed that he excavated the hermit's cave in the cliff on the south side of the valley in the first half of the twelfth century, and his holy influence led to several attempts to establish monastic life in the area, which were finally successful with the arrival of the Premonstratensian Order in about 1200.

A Victorian history of Dale by John Ward[75] stresses the wild and isolated nature of the district:

> *We know nothing of Dale, or as it was anciently called, Depedale, previous to this period [the twelfth century], beyond that it was a marshy and lonely place in the midst of an expanse of woodland from Derby to the Erewash, unbroken except for a few scattered villages.*

In fact, by this period neither hermits nor monks were necessarily associated with wilderness. As Ward goes on to point out (of hermits):

> *Their substantial little houses were usually placed where they could be of some service to their fellow men, especially to travellers, as by a bridge, a ford, a marsh, or at the meeting of ways in some dense forest....*[76]

Dreams of prophetic instruction are a common feature of medieval religious culture, and it seems far more likely that the baker from Derby actually chose to live close to the line of the Portway, where the cliff face provided shelter and where guidance to travellers might have been needed on the steep incline.

Later in the century the monks might also have seen the advantage of a site on an ancient line of communication, since they were becoming less concerned with sacred solitude than with encouraging pilgrimage and the income to be gained from it. Dale may not have been in the same league for pilgrims as Canterbury or Walsingham, but at the time of the Dissolution of the Monasteries in 1539 it is recorded as possessing relics associated with its patron St Mary, such as a girdle and some milk. It would have been a day's journey from either Derby or Nottingham: an ideal short pilgrimage for those needing the kind of cure or assistance St Mary might provide.

According to James Pilkington:[77] 'there used to be a tradition that all travellers and strangers were entertained and lodged at the abbey for one night, and in the morning given supplies for their journey, which suggests that the monastic obligation to provide hospitality was not neglected at Dale'. Presumably the bulk of these guests were long-distance users of the Portway.

Today Dale is a distinctly up-market village, which has come a long way from the habitation of lowly monks and hermits. Despite this, it still has an air of seclusion, protected on the south by the sandstone scarp. The surviving arch of the east window of the abbey church gives an idea of the scale of the monastery buildings, but it is one of the few traces of the substantial original structure to remain, much of the stone having been robbed to build (among other places) Risley Hall. Although the abbey was endowed with about 24,000 acres and was one of the richest in Derbyshire, there were only between 16 and 20 monks attached to it. It seems likely that much of the day-to-day work was carried out by laymen.

The most interesting building in Dale is now All Saints Church, which was possibly once part of the abbey, but more likely the chapel of Depedale. Pevsner[78] calls it 'one of the smallest and oddest of English churches', not only on account of its size, but because it is attached to a house on its west side, making it a very unusual semi-detached church. Inside it is only about eight metres square, and feels very crowded with box pews. Among its treasures are some fragments of thirteenth-century wall paintings. The adjoining house was for many years a pub called the Blue Bell.

WALKING : THE HEMLOCK STONE TO DALE (ABOUT 4½ MILES)

From Bramcote Hills Park the route crosses Ilkeston Road and follows Hicking Lane, which continues in the same southwesterly direction into the centre of Stapleford. The lane, lined with mainly 1950s semi-detached houses, shows signs of having once been a rural route, as there are fragments of old hedges in places. Crossing Church Street and turning left, the river Erewash can be reached via Manor Avenue or Mill Road on the right. (The church and cross can be found a little further down the street.) These run through an area of Edwardian terraced houses, and lead to the Old Mill.

Cross the river by the steel bridge and follow the track to the railway footbridge. Beyond this, take the stone bridge over the canal and then bear left over the meadows, which have clear ridge and furrow marks, to Stanton Gate Road. This must be a relatively new road, as it is not shown on the OS map of 1896. (If the meadows are very wet it is also possible to go straight ahead by an alternative path.) Cross the road and then go uphill across another pasture to join a well-defined old track at the base of the scarp, worn into the rock as a distinct holloway [hollow way], which comes out by St Giles Church in Sandiacre.

Leave the churchyard on the south side and follow Church Drive downhill, turning right onto Stanton Road. After crossing the M1 the pavement gives out and it is road walking until Dale. The busy road from Stanton to Risley is crossed, and then the road climbs past a large house on the right called The Hewarths. 'Heworth' is a name mentioned in the thirteenth-century charter. This stretch is called No Man's Lane both on the map and on road signs.

After going steadily northwest for about a mile the road swings sharply right and widens out at a pair of Victorian cottages. It is then downhill walking as far as the right-angle bend at Boyah Grange. Turn right here along Potato Pit Lane before coming to a footpath on the left. Take this and head northwest, skirting the hollows, and continue on the footpath through the next meadow and then across arable land. This leads to Hermit's Wood, a narrow belt of woodland on the scarp face. Various steep paths drop down through the wood, and the hermitage can be found in the cliff face.

Follow the main track at the base of the cliff west to the church, and then turn north by the churchyard and go through the gate, which leads into the village street. This bends to the right, and at the end of the street turn left at the Carpenter's Arms to leave the village by the steep Arbour Hill. If preferred, road walking can be avoided by taking a field path out of the village street parallel to the road, which runs to the southwest of the wooded summit of Arbour Hill.

C. DALE TO COXBENCH

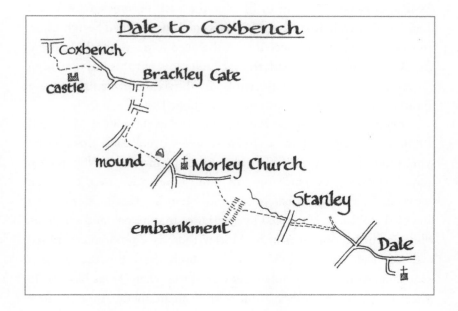

The name of Arbour Hill, which dominates the road west out of Dale, may be derived from the Celtic word *arrhber*, a fortress, according to Ward.[79] This is the second Arbour Hill on the route, and could well have been a fortified campsite established for the benefit of travellers. This would mean that they were not created to 'control' the road, as has been suggested, but rather to shelter road users.

Beyond the Ilkeston Road, the line of the Portway from Upper Hagg Farm to the church at Morley has been obscured by the building of the 1878 GNR railway between Derby Friargate and Nottingham, and the development of Stanley Kilbourne Colliery. From Upper Hagg the most likely route is the track running west downhill towards Lower Hagg, which soon descends to quite boggy ground where 'coal pits' are marked on Sanderson's map, which were still marked as

Kilbourne Colliery on the 1896 OS map. It seems that these were quite shallow coal deposits, and today little trace remains of the workings. As it approaches the road to Stanley the path becomes a track and then is called Dale Road, but 100 years ago it was named Sough Lane. This may have been connected with the need to de-water the colliery. The Bridge Inn used to mark the road junction, but this has now been converted into a private house, with only the signboard remaining as a reminder of its former incarnation as a public house.

This next section of the Portway to Morley church (St Matthew) is unusual in that it follows a stream (Stanley Brook) and crosses low-lying ground, which must have been swampy in winter. Nonetheless quite convincing evidence for this route is provided by the section between the railway embankment and Church Lane in Morley. The line of the old lane is marked by a series of mature oak and ash trees, while in the section nearest to Morley there is a pronounced raised roadbed. The maps of 1835 and 1896 both show this section as a wide lane, which presumably went out of use when it was blocked to wheeled vehicles by construction of the embankment. An alternative route, which crossed the railway on a bridge near Stanley, would then have replaced the original track. This final section of the lane up to the church is particularly attractive, with a vigorous stream running beside the road on the left.

Morley churchyard is a peaceful place with a mausoleum and two crosses as well as the rectory, a tithe barn and the church itself. The latter contains an important collection of stained glass from Dale Abbey, removed at the time of the Dissolution. The south porch is also believed to have come from the same source. Pevsner[80] says of the glass: 'enough remains to make Morley the most rewarding place in the country to study late medieval stained glass'. One cross, the Butter Cross, has an ancient stepped base with a modern (early twentieth-century) carved shaft, and is located on what used to be a village green. The other is shortened, with a sundial placed on top. Although the church is dedicated to St Matthew, it may be significant that the patron saint of the Lords of Morley was St Christopher, associated with travellers.

One striking feature of the church is the height of the spire, which may have served as a useful landmark for travellers on this relatively flat section of the Portway. The wealth displayed in the church contrasts with the small size and dispersed nature of the modern village. But it had a

Butter Cross in St Matthew's churchyard, Morley.

strategic position at the junction of two major ancient routes: the Portway and Ryknild Street – the important Roman road which ran from the Cotswolds to Chesterfield and beyond. The position of Breadsall Priory (now a hotel) a mile west of the church may also be significant, since good transport links would have been important to the Austin (Augustinian) canons who founded the priory in the thirteenth century.

In an article in the *Derbyshire Archaeological Journal* of 1912, Percy Currey[81] describes an old route from the Bottle Brook to Dale:

Mr. John Ward, in 'Dale and its Abbey', speaks of travellers between Derby and Nottingham going through Stanley Park, and this road would give an almost straight connection between Duffield Bridge and Nottinghamshire by the same route. On Morley Moor the road takes a sharp bend round the well-known moated mound. Whether the bend in the road fixed the site of the mound, or whether the mound fixed the line of the road, is hard to say, but there is an obvious connection between the two which is proof of great antiquity.

He is referring to the Mound, a semi-moated site containing a man-made hill about six metres high, which appears to be sited on the exact line of the Portway. Just beyond the main road the track makes a sharp bend to skirt round the obstacle which, in summer, is almost invisible under its tree cover. Apparently not a barrow, there is no agreement on the function or age of the Mound, which is clearly too small to be defensive. One theory is that it was a survey point for constructing the nearby Ryknild Street. It is interesting to note that near here there is a significant change of direction in the Roman road, from northeast to nearly due north, and the mound is in alignment with the northern stretch. Another possibility is that it was the meeting place for the Morleyston and Litchurch Hundred. There may have actually been a marker stone on the mound, and of course the Portway would have made travelling to any meeting there much easier.

Beyond the Mound the track is bounded by a thick, mainly holly hedge on the south side, which may be growing on the original route. From Morleymoor the direct route northwest to Coxbench involves dropping into the steep valley of the Carr Brook. Although this direction can be followed on footpaths and tracks, it seems more likely that the ancient route turned to the north to stay on higher ground. It is also possible that after Ryknild Street was constructed, travellers used that route from Morleymoor to Brackley Gate and there turned west.

The road junction at Horsley Farm Park is an interesting example of the changes that can occur in the road pattern over a relatively short period. The present surfaced road (Sandy Lane) running down towards Horsley only dates from 1865, when the old lane to the left was blocked by the growth of quarrying. This was known as Park Lane, and is shown on Sanderson's 1835 map, Horsley Park being the wide area to the north and south of Horsley (or Horeston) Castle, originally a hunting ground for the landowner. This beautiful track is, in part, a ridgeway, and has views far to the north, with Alport Height again visible on the horizon.

Morley Mound with the spire of St Matthew's in the distance.

Today almost nothing remains of the castle, which was apparently built in the eleventh century. The whole site is thickly wooded and full of hummocks, although it is possible to see fragments of a few masonry walls. One story is that the stone was removed in the eighteenth century to build Kedleston Hall, though this may refer to stone taken from the nearby quarry. As is often the case, there is little surviving evidence about the form or use of the castle. The medieval castle could have been built on the site of a prehistoric stronghold, possibly another encampment for long-distance travellers.

Evidence for this section of the route being pre-medieval is provided through the finding by two quarrymen of a Roman coin dating from 103 CE, with some pottery fragments.[82] Another curious aspect of this locality is that the castle area used to be famous for its display of daffodils, and what is now a deserted wood was once something of a tourist attraction, with the farm offering teas.

The presence of the A38, noisy on its embankment as it passes through Coxbench, makes it hard to imagine this valley when the Portway was the main route. The OS map of 1896 makes it clear how dramatically the landscape here has been affected by industrialisation. Before the modern road there was both a tramway and a railway, the latter including a spur into Coxbench quarry, which may have provided the main employment locally.

To the east of the track, near the kennels, is a tree-covered mound, not moated like the one at Morley, which seems man-made. According to Davies[83] it is 'a large circular mound rising to a considerable elevation which appears to be an ancient tumulus. The old people call it "The Devil's Shovel-ful"'. Because it is so close to the new road, and covered with trees, the mound is no longer as prominent as it once must have been, but its proximity to the Portway may nonetheless be significant.

At the bottom of the track, practically underneath the A38 flyover, is the stone canopy of St Anthony's Well, with a notice saying that it has been moved from an (unspecified) cottage garden. According to Doris Howe,[84] Coxbench was previously known as St Anthony's Cross, which may have marked the junction of the Portway with another route running up the valley of the Bottle Brook. St Anthony was noted for being an early hermit and ascetic, but why he should be connected with this spot is unclear, unless there was a hermitage nearby.

St. Anthony's Well, Coxbench.

WALKING: DALE TO COXBENCH (ABOUT 7 MILES)

Leaving Dale, at the top of Arbour Hill is the road between Spondon and Ilkeston. Cross this and continue along the asphalt lane (Hagg Lane) to Upper Hagg Farm. Turn west downhill past Lower Hagg Farm, and then by a field track which becomes Dale Road. Cross the road to Stanley by the old Bridge Inn. On the west side of the road the path continues beside the brook, crossing several meadows. The path then forks, with one branch running north to Stanley. Avoid this, which crosses the brook, and instead head northwest, keeping the hedge on the left, towards the disused railway embankment, which here is covered by a belt of trees. Cross the embankment, beyond which the route is marked by an occasional line of oak and ash trees, before joining Church Lane about half a mile below Morley church.

Follow Lime Lane from the church to the main road (A608), cross this and look for an unmarked stile opposite. Join the track running northwest. Beyond the Mound (discussed above) the track continues into Morleymoor and past the Sacheverell Almshouses of 1656, which are the most interesting feature of this part of the village.

However, at Morleymoor the best walking route is instead to turn north onto a well-defined track just before entering the village. This runs beside an area of boggy woodland on the left, and is roughly parallel to the old Ryknild Street. After crossing Brick Kiln Lane it continues to Morleymoor Farm, an attractive redbrick house with deep sash windows, after which a field path crosses the pasture to emerge onto the road at Brackley Gate. The route then turns west to Brackley Gate Farm, after which the road – Sandy Lane – drops down, but it still provides good views to the north towards Horsley. Take the unmade road on the left to Horsley Park Farm.

The site of Horsley Castle is on the left in Castle Wood, obscured by the covering of trees. Beyond the castle the line of the original route is blocked by a chain link fence protecting a quarried area, which has clearly obliterated what may have been a direct route to Holbrook. The path now turns right to skirt this old quarry and descends to the A38 flyover at Coxbench beside some kennels.

D. COXBENCH TO ALPORT HEIGHT

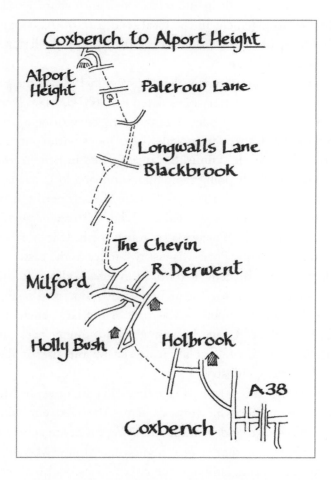

The next section of road, leading uphill to the village of Holbrook, is unique as it is actually called 'Portway' on OS maps as well as on roadside signs, a remarkable survival and the only section of the entire route to be thus marked. According to Howe[85] there is a documentary record of 'Le Portway at Holbrook' from 1596. Despite this, tracing the route from Holbrook to the Derwent crossing is difficult. It may well have gone through what are now the grounds of Holbrook Hall, since when this was built in the mid-seventeenth century there was probably a re-arrangement in the local road pattern. Although there are several footpaths branching off from the road on the left, none go in the direction of Makeney.

What is surely significant is the discovery in 1962, in the grounds of the Hall, of several pottery kilns dated to 170 CE.[86] Two have been excavated, and the main product seems to have been storage jars of the type used by the Romans to provide their troops with containers for basic rations. The second kiln is the largest found in Britain from this period, so it was clearly doing more than supplying local needs; pieces of this pottery have been found at Roman sites in northern Britain. The jars may have been transported on Ryknild Street, or possibly the Romans used the older Portway as a route north. It is worth noting that the modern Denby Pottery is just two miles to the east.

Holbrook church, dedicated to St Michael, dates from 1841, replacing a chapel of 1761. The arched east window and pedimented belfry are distinctive. Holbrook was part of the large ancient parish of Duffield until 1863, but the new church building here probably reflected the growth of population caused by the rise of the local framework knitting industry.

After passing through the village the field path down to Makeney offers tremendous views northwards across the Derwent valley: the Chevin in the foreground with the surveying tower are clearly visible, with Alport Height in the distance. Somewhere around Makeney there must have been a ford, although the river's course will have changed so much over the past thousand years or so that finding the precise location is impossible. According to Kenneth Cameron,[87] medieval Makeney was a more important settlement than Milford, possibly as a consequence of the Portway. On Peter Burdett's map Milford is not even marked and there is no bridge, since the settlement was essentially developed by the Strutt family of Belper after 1780.

The Hollybush Inn, Makeney.

The name nonetheless clearly suggests a ford near here, and as the name in the Domesday Book is 'Muleford', this was possibly the one used by the Portway, on which mules would have been common pack animals. The 1896 OS map shows a suggestive length of causeway on the far side of the river, just north of Moscow Farm, which can still be seen near the edge of a field to the west of the A6, just past Milford House. This might have led to a ford opposite Makeney Hall, and is in approximate alignment with the field path above the Holly Bush pub. This well-known inn, which claims to be one of the oldest in the county, appears to be right on the line of the Portway, and is one of two with this name on the route. It is also worth noting that the 'holly bush' was one of the earliest emblems adopted for inn signs.

Milford today is a pretty village above the A6, with the cottages of former millworkers banked up the slope. It is built at the southern end of the Chevin – a Celtic name meaning ridge – and this is the main landscape feature here on the west side of the Derwent, reaching a height of 190 metres.

In this section the line of the Portway appears clear; it must have followed the crest of the Chevin northwards, along what is today North Lane. This is a wide, tree-lined track, with good views in places towards Belper on the far side of the Derwent. A railway tunnel on the Derby–Sheffield line – originally the North Midland Railway (1840) – runs under the Chevin near Milford. This explains the ruined tower at the top of Sunny Hill, which was built to align the tunnel works (engineered by George Stephenson) and to make sure the tunnellers from each end met in the middle. An airshaft can be seen in the field on the opposite side of the track.

The first section of the lane is bounded by a golf course, and in the middle part on the east side is a massive stone wall, about seven metres high and set at an angle to the track, which was apparently built as a shooting range in the nineteenth century.

Longwalls Lane above Blackbrook.

From the junction with Farnah Green Road the original line of the way to Blackbrook is lost, blocked by a substantial house. But the alternative route is almost entirely on good footpaths along the Lumb Brook valley. At Blackbrook, Longwalls Lane appears to resume the route of the Portway, climbing steadily and then steeply out of the hamlet. In places the floor of the track consists of large slabs of bedrock, which suggests erosion caused by heavy use. To the east of the lane, in the grounds of Starbuck House, a Romano-British quern manufacturing site has been recently discovered.[88] These were small millstones about 35cms across; essentially, portable flour mills. It seems likely that this site was chosen because the Portway offered convenient transport facilities for the finished querns towards both north and south, presumably carried by packhorse.

Further on the lane levels out and offers good views on both sides. Looking back south beyond Blackbrook, a belt of trees and the line of field boundaries running up the hillside seems to be close to the lost line of the Portway. In the other direction, towards the lane's end, Alport Height is clearly visible to the northwest, while there are several footpaths crossing the route. The wood on the east side has the suggestive name of Streets Wood, and the place where the lane joins Wilderbrook Lane is known as Knaves Cross.[89] The origin of

Alport Height from the top of Longwalls Lane.

103

this name is obscure, but it may have referred to a wayside cross or, ironically, a gibbet.

Alport Height, a significant route marker, is now only two miles away, and a well-defined footpath runs almost straight uphill across the fields from Wilderbrook Lane, following the highest ground and offering wonderful views, especially south over the Trent valley. This is empty country, over 250 metres high, bleak enough even in summer, with swallows swooping over the grassland and a kestrel hovering near Crowtrees Farm.

Compared with the other side of the Derwent there is a noticeable lack of villages on this plateau; in fact, only hamlets are passed between Milford and Wirksworth. The existence and survival of the footpath in such an isolated area, and its orientation to Alport Height, is another indicator of the considerable age of the route.

The prominence of Alport Height (314m) is exaggerated now by the radio masts on the top, but even without these it would have been a useful landmark. From the car park there are splendid views south and west, with Shropshire visible on a clear day. However, it is worth noting that the prominent stone pillar on the west face of the hill must have been created by quarrying and cannot be an ancient feature. Yet the name clearly links the Portway to the hilltop, which has been sporadically visible along the route since Sandiacre. The summit has been owned by the National Trust since 1930, and a guide stoop can be found there which Smith[90] believes originally stood at the road junction of Alport Lane and Back Lane, just below the Height. This one only shows three directions: Wirksworth, Derby and Ashbourne, and reinforces the idea that this route was still of some importance early in the eighteenth century.

WALKING: COXBENCH TO ALPORT HEIGHT (ABOUT 8 MILES)

Picking up the route where the track runs down from Castle Wood to meet the A38, turn left under the flyover, then cross straight over the B679 and the track of the old railway and turn right past Coxbench Hall. Fork left after a few hundred metres and continue uphill towards Holbrook: there is a pavement all the way. As the line of the Portway is obscure here, the best route through the village is to take Mellors Lane to the left and follow this past the playground to the junction with Makeney Road. (This used to be the main turnpike road between Derby and Sheffield, and a toll collector's cottage can be seen a short distance downhill.) A little to the left of the junction a field path can be found on the right which runs downhill to Makeney, to emerge by the steps above the Holly Bush pub. Turn right at the pub and follow the road towards Milford. There are excellent views of the weirs below Milford Bridge, built for the now-demolished mills. This brings you out on the A6 by the King William IV pub.

Cross the bridge and take Chevin Road on the right to a road on the left called Sunny Hill, which climbs steeply to North Lane. This runs along the top of the Chevin for about a mile. At the far end the lane abruptly swings west and joins the road at Farnah Green. This diversion is shown on the map of 1835 and may have been caused by the building of Chevin Mount, the large house on this site. From here to Blackbrook (over half a mile) the line of the Portway is again unclear, but the best walking route is to turn briefly right into Farnah Green Road, then take a track to the left, but soon turning right along the top of the wooded Lumb Brook valley. After another right turn this track fords the stream and then emerges at Blackbrook, only a hundred yards from the end of Longwalls Lane (here part of the Midshires Way).

Longwalls Lane runs north for over a mile before reaching the junction of Knaves Cross. Turn left here downhill onto Wilderbrook Lane for a short distance and then note the path signed on the right. The bottom corner of this field can be very wet, so it is better to walk a little further on the lane and then go through the gate on the right and head for the stile opposite. From here there should be no difficulty in following the track, as it is marked by a succession of squeeze stiles.

There is a small wood by the crossing of Palerow Lane, which takes its name from the pale, or fence which used to surround the huge medieval deer park which stretched from here to Duffield. The next section is not well marked, and it is worth keeping the map handy until you are past Coneygreave Farm, on the left. The path emerges at the meeting of Peat Lane and Back Lane. Follow the latter to the east of the hilltop and the next road junction. The summit of Alport Height can be reached by turning left from here.

E. ALPORT HEIGHT TO WINSTER

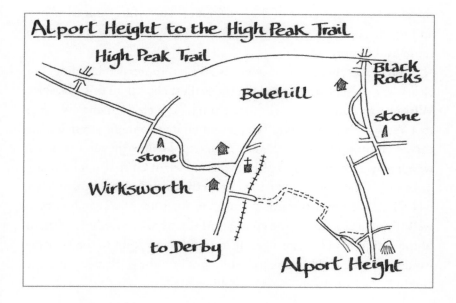

Less than two miles from Alport Height, Wirksworth is a characterful town which sits at the head of the Ecclesbourne valley. This name may mean 'the stream of the church' (*egles* is Celtic for church), indicating the early importance of the town and suggesting that the church may have been founded in the Romano-British period. In fact, the church in Wirksworth (dedicated to St Mary) is sited very close to the source of the River Ecclesbourne. Today it is notable that, unlike other Derbyshire towns, Wirksworth is not on a main road; therefore it is possible that in the past the Portway provided the main routes to north and south.

It has been claimed that Wirksworth was at the centre of Roman lead production in the Peak District: the much-discussed lost town of Lutudarum.[91] Whatever the truth of this, there is little doubt that lead was mined and processed here before, during and after the Roman period. The wealth generated by this industrial activity could have supported church building at an early date. Much later, during the sixteenth century, Wirksworth was the second most important town in the county, an indication of the continuing value of its mineral riches, and the Moot Hall, now in Chapel Lane, was the seat of a court to settle lead mining disputes.

Today the church of St Mary is still an impressive building, but clearly the present structure is not the earliest church on this site, since Wirksworth had an early minster church, as well as giving its name to a Viking-era wapentake. The present church contains a remarkable carved coffin lid from c. 700–800 CE, found below the altar in 1820, which may mark the burial place of an important Christian missionary or bishop. One legend links it to St Betti, an early Saxon missionary who died in the mid-seventh century, but there are other candidates as well.[92] The oval shape of the churchyard is said to be another indicator of the antiquity of the site. Clearly its position adjacent to the Portway would have allowed lead ore to be brought into the settlement, and the nearby village of Bolehill was a smelting site.[93]

'Stands the church clock at ten to three?' St Mary's Church, Wirksworth.

The Romans were certainly keen to increase lead production to satisfy their industrial and domestic needs, and a pig of lead was found north of Wirksworth in 1777 with a Latin inscription dating to the reign of Hadrian.[94] However, very little other evidence has been found from this period, and it may be that this was originally more of an industrial area than a town *per se*. (A fuller discussion of Wirksworth in the Roman period is provided in Anton Shone's *Origins and History of Wirksworth*.[95])

In its initial phase as a prehistoric trackway, the Portway would have avoided the low-lying site of the future town, and so would have looped around the valley to the east and the north. (This was also the route adopted much later, in the eighteenth century, for the Alfreton to Ashbourne turnpike.) Evidential support for this early route is provided by the standing stone in the field to the east of the Malt Shovel pub, and the name Porter Lane for the stretch of the B5035 between the Cromford and Middleton roads.

When Wirksworth began to develop, first as a mining area and later as a religious centre and market, some travellers would have wanted to leave the old track and descend into the town. One likely route from Alport Height is via Prathall Lane to Gorseybank, then into the centre by St John's Street. Leaving the town on the other side via West End and Brassington Lane, the long climb up from the market place is marked by a standing stone above Norbreck Farm.

Climbing out of the town, the walker is immediately aware of a new sense of bleakness and emptiness, in contrast to the softer, leafier landscape to the south. This is the first section of the Portway in the White Peak (i.e. on limestone). There are fewer trees and farms, and settlement is generally more dispersed. Perhaps because of this, the man-made scars linked to stone quarrying and lead mining seem more obvious, while the giant wind turbines on Carsington Pastures turn slowly in the breeze.

The landscape of this area between Wirksworth and Brassington was considerably altered by the construction of the Cromford and

High Peak Railway after 1826, and then by the quarrying which was initially encouraged by the railway. A curious feature of this railway is that it was originally planned as a canal, railways being unproven at that date. The route was therefore planned in canal style, either on the level or on steep inclines (which would, incredibly, have been flights of locks), such as the slope leading up to Middleton Top. On Sanderson's 1835 map all the stations are labelled 'wharves'.

There is much debate about the likely course of the Portway just west of Wirksworth. As mentioned above, quarrying, the railway and also the construction of the Via Gellia road for Philip Gell of Hopton Hall in 1791 have all contributed to obscuring the ancient road pattern. A strong case has been made that the Street and the Portway joined near Harborough Rocks to the north of Wirksworth, and then continued on down into the town, but the exact route may never be agreed.[96]

From Harborough Rocks the route of the Portway is much clearer. Burdett's map shows it running directly from here to Grangemill. However, a large dusty quarry has obliterated the southern end, so to join the route it is necessary to take the path just past the old Hopton Station, which runs northwest to Griffe Grange. This name gives a clue to the nature of the area: before the quarries, the limestone hills were found to be ideal for grazing sheep, which led to the establishment of large monastic farms known as granges. In the medieval period Griffe Grange belonged to Dale Abbey, to which it was directly linked by the Portway.

Although not densely settled today, in prehistoric times this area may have supported a larger population, judging by the wealth of prehistoric features. The most distinctive of these are the 'lows': Ivet Low, Minninglow, Green Low and Slipper Low are all in the locality. Confusingly, the name seems to come from the Old English *hlaw*, meaning hill or mound, often used for burials.

The section of the Portway between Harborough and Grangemill was known as the Chariot Way, an unlikely name which may however derive from the Old English prefix *cerring*, a bend in a road. The bend

Cave at Harborough Rocks

here marked the change in direction from west to northwest. Before the Via Gellia was built this was a principal route from Derby to the northwest, and was called the Old Manchester Road. Today it is a broad white track, surfaced with limestone chippings, running mainly downhill from its highest point of over 300 metres. The views from here are spectacular; a farmer told me that the Wrekin is sometimes visible, over 50 miles away. The Trent valley seems much nearer, with the line of the river marked by several steaming sets of cooling towers.

To the west, Harborough Rocks dominate the skyline, although they look more impressive from the High Peak Trail, from where the natural limestone turrets are more prominent. On the northwest side of the Rocks is a cave which was inhabited when Daniel Defoe visited in 1720. He described being shown round by the woman who lived there with her lead miner husband and five children:

> *... we alighted and went in: There was a large hollow cave, which the poor people by two curtains hang'd cross, had parted into three rooms. On one*

side was the chimney, and the man, or perhaps his father, being miners, had found means to work a shaft or funnel through the rock to carry the smoke out at the top, where the giant's tombstone was. The habitation was poor, 'tis true, but things within did not look so like misery as I had expected. Every thing was clean and neat, tho' mean and ordinary.....[97]

Today the idea of living in the dripping wet cave seems incredible, although the chimney can still be seen. However, a series of excavations carried out on this site have found evidence of habitation dating back to the Bronze Age, although the latest published report[98] describes the area as an Iron Age settlement. The archaeological finds include late Bronze Age and Iron Age pottery as well as quantities of animal bones: ox, sheep and pig. The bulk of the finds occurred on the northeastern side of the site, which is all on Access Land. At 379 metres the summit around the trig point, marked by a series of teeth-like rocks, offers spectacular views in all directions, from the High Peak to the north and on over Carsington Water looking southwards. The idea of an encampment here to offer shelter to travellers is supported by the probability that it marked the junction of two important ancient routes.

Returning to the main route, between Harborough Rocks and the Portway lies New Harboro Farm, an isolated group of buildings. Griffe Walk Farm is next on the left, and half a mile past this the line of the old route is blocked by the spread of Grange Mill Quarry, invisible but audible with the steady roar of heavy machines and the irritating beep of reversing trucks.

The settlement of Grangemill consists of the Holly Bush pub, a furniture workshop, a farm and the old mill building, with its large millpond. The pond is fed by the stream which runs down the east side of the Winster road and presumably originates at Shothouse Spring, a constant source of water about halfway up the valley. There is apparently a distinct *aggar* (the platform of a Roman road) running up the west side of the valley above the line of the present road, although this is on private land. Excavation carried out near here by the Wirksworth Roman Project[99] has revealed the structure of two successive Roman road surfaces here. Another feature of this stretch is the outline of a possible Roman camp[100] just north of Wigleymeadow Farm.

Given the spring and the likely boggy nature of the valley, it is possible that in prehistoric times the best route north was along the 300 metres contour to the east, which can be followed by taking the field path from Whitelow Farm towards Winster. This route, although not a ridgeway, gives the traveller excellent views north and west, including sight of Robin Hood's Stride directly ahead. Evidence of an older road pattern is provided by a guide stoop in the fields near Winstermoor Farm, indicating the directions of Chesterfield, Bakewell, Ashbourne and Matlock.[101] This contrasts with a neighbouring guide stoop[102] near the start of Bonsall Lane on the west side of the B5056 (now acting as a gatepost), which is labelled Leek, Bonsall, Bakewell and Wirksworth. These guide stoops reveal a fluid road pattern in an area that must have been uncultivated moor in the early eighteenth century: clearly a vanished road ran northeast from Shothouse Spring, on a line still marked by a parish boundary.

The Portway passes between the settlements of Elton and Winster. The latter is an attractive village and well worth a detour, although walkers will again realise why the old route kept to the higher ground: visiting the village involves a very steep descent.

WALKING: ALPORT HEIGHT TO THE HIGH PEAK TRAIL (4 OR 5 MILES, DEPENDING ON ROUTE)

(1) The ancient route, skirting around Wirksworth (about 5 miles)

From the crossroads near Alport Height take Alport Lane northwest, which becomes Hay Lane. Part of this gently curving road is a holloway. Fork right into Breamfield Lane, which emerges near Moor Farm onto the old turnpike road to Belper. Turn left, cross over the road down to Whatstandwell and go past the Malt Shovel pub onto Oakerthorpe Road. Note the standing stone in the field opposite. Oakerthorpe Road appears to be an enclosure road as it runs dead straight for half a mile. At the junction on the left take the lane down into Bolehill. This route has been closed to through traffic, which makes for more pleasant walking, but the original course of the Portway is more likely to have been on the contour line above. From Bolehill village walk up towards Black Rocks, where the construction of the High Peak Railway clearly had a major impact on the landscape. The simplest and most pleasant route from here is to join the High Peak trail at Black Rocks car park and follow it west past Middleton Top engine house to reach the old station for Hopton village.

(2) The later route through the town of Wirksworth (about 4 miles)

From the Alport Height crossroads go west downhill for half a mile. Take the path marked down the slope on the right, which joins Taylor's Lane and leads to Holehouse Farm. From here a green though usually muddy track, Prathall Lane, leads to Gorseybank. Cross the railway and continue towards the B5023, the main road to Derby. Take this into the centre of Wirksworth, where the secluded church and churchyard can be found behind the shops on the right, with the old market place to the left. Turn left here up West End, until half a mile above the market place the route forks right and continues along the fringe of an old quarry. Follow this fork past the ruins of several small field barns and the standing stone on the left as far as the crossroads with the road for Carsington. Turn right and then left very shortly after, and follow the Brassington road B5035 west until it is possible to join the High Peak Trail, so joining up with the first route above.

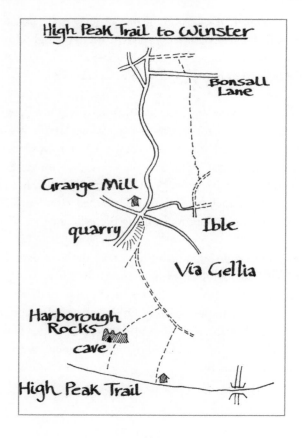

FROM THE HIGH PEAK TRAIL
TO WINSTER (ABOUT 5 MILES)

Continue on the trail past the quarry to the house which was once the station for Hopton and Carsington. A bridleway is signposted to the right. Take this until it joins the original line of the Portway after half a mile, where you turn left. To make a detour to Harborough Rocks, take the footpath to the left at New Harboro Farm, going to the right of the farmhouse and then up the hill. The cave will be found on the far side.

Back on the main track continue for about a mile and at the T-junction by the screen of trees take the path to the right that runs down across several sloping meadows, before joining up with the old track just before Grangemill and the Via Gellia.

At the junction cross the Via Gellia (A5012) onto the Winster road. This road is quite busy and rather narrow, making for unpleasant walking, so a more comfortable alternative is to take the right turn at Grangemill, signposted Ible, and walk uphill for half a mile, past Tophill Farm to the crossroads near the deserted Whitelow Farm. Turn left here, and a hundred yards beyond the farm a path is signposted to the left. This runs for over a mile through numerous stiles to Bonsall Lane.

Turn left onto Bonsall Lane and then take the next path on the right, which leads uphill to meet the track which is now part of the Limestone Way. To visit Winster there is a path down on the opposite side of the Limestone Way. Otherwise, turn left and follow the track to the B5056, cross the road, and walk west for a few yards before meeting the unsurfaced Islington Lane running north. At this point the Miners Standard pub is conveniently close, if a break is desired.

F. WINSTER TO ASHFORD-IN-THE-WATER

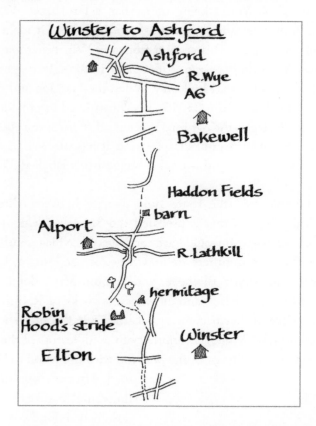

Winster derives its quiet elegance from lead-mining wealth, but above the village, where the Portway runs along Islington Lane, the landscape feels rather bedraggled. The name Islington Lane refers to the lost village of Islington, which was a shanty town for itinerant miners, and is shown on Peter Burdett's map as a hamlet. Even now it is apparent that this was mining country: spoil heaps and ruined buildings abound, small compounds full of weeds and junk, rusting vehicles and thistles giving a somewhat desolate feel to the landscape over a century after the industry was played out.

The lane is unsurfaced, although in places the layer of polished stones gives it the feel of being more than a farm track. With tall hedges on both sides and frequent ash and oak trees it makes for a shady walk in summer. This section from the Winster crossroads to Robin Hood's Stride is easy to follow and is strongly suggestive of an ancient road, being part holloway. When the Haddon and Bentley Turnpike of 1811 (now the B5056) was constructed to provide easier gradients for carriages, the old road was cut off to force travellers onto the new route, but instead of disappearing, it has survived as a green lane. On Sanderson's map this track is suggestively labelled 'Porteway Lane'.

It is notable that the route runs directly between Elton and Winster. This suggests that it predated the Saxon settlement of the region, since otherwise it would have connected the villages rather than by-passing them. In fact there are no villages on the Portway between Wirksworth and Alport. Birchover and Stanton Moor dominate the landscape to the northeast, and at times the rocks of Robin Hood's Stride are visible as they become closer. The 1896 OS map shows the site of the Portaway Mine,[103] – another of the indicators of the route's existence – to the northeast of the junction with the Elton to Winster road. After crossing this road, the route is surfaced and is now called Dudwood Lane. Where this rejoins the main road there is a gated track in front which leads up quite steeply through a meadow towards the pinnacles of Robin Hood's Stride, with Cratcliff Rocks on the right.

Nine Stone Circle, Harthill Moor.

The area around Robin Hood's Stride is known

as Harthill Moor and is particularly rich in prehistoric and historic remains. Robin Hood was a versatile character and has given his name to many landscape features in the North Midlands, and this name is probably medieval. (An alternative is Mock Beggar's Hall.) The gritstone crags would have certainly acted as a distinctive landmark for users of the Portway, and there appears to be evidence of deliberate working on them, either for quarrying or to emphasise their outline.

Among the features which are clearly manmade are the enclosure on Cratcliff Rocks, which may be late Neolithic, the circle at Nine Stone Close, which has also been given a tentative Neolithic date, at least one tumulus, and the Castle Ring hillfort. None of these can be dated accurately, and they may have been in use at different periods. For example, the enclosure at Castle Ring to the northwest of Harthill Moor Farm might have been a replacement of the earlier stronghold on Cratcliff Rocks. Either would have provided a secure camping place for travellers. It is curious that the Nine Stone Circle (five of them are missing) was composed of the same number as the Nine Ladies Circle, which is only two miles to the east on Stanton Moor.

The most recently discovered feature here is an example of cup-and-ring art, an art form normally linked to the early Bronze Age, which was found on the base of a boulder. A possible link between these carvings and the Portway has been suggested in an article by Graeme Guilbert *et al*.:

> ... *recent theories have sought to demonstrate that the siting of some prehistoric rock art may be explicable in terms of marking significant points along contemporary routes through the landscape*...[104]

The same article presents a full analysis of the prehistoric features of the area.

The hermitage cave found at the west end of Cratcliff Rocks is probably less ancient. The carved crucifix is thought to be medieval,

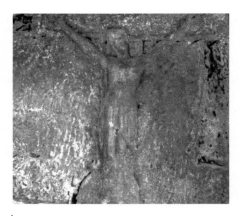

Carved crucifix in the hermitage at Cratcliff Rocks.

while the records of Haddon Hall for 1550 mention paying a hermit 8d for providing rabbits.[105] This is the fourth hermitage on the Portway, and as R.W.P. Cockerton notes:

> ... *it may be that the good man was able to be of assistance to travellers and performed the duties of an unofficial guide, but his choice of a hermitage can hardly have been dictated by a desire for enduring solitude.*[106]

Clearly an effort has been made to protect the cave and carving by installing some railings, and a pair of yew trees have also been planted in order to distinguish the site, though they now look somewhat forlorn.

Although the prominence of Robin Hood's Stride has been reduced by the growth of the belt of conifers to the south, the view from the top in all directions is still remarkable, and this would undoubtedly have been an asset to any defensive site near here. The line of ancient sweet chestnut trees on the south side of the enclosure, which marks a parish boundary, is also worth noting, as this tree is uncommon in the Peak District.

It seems hard to believe today, but according to Cockerton,[107] in the seventeenth century the 'common highway' from Manchester to Derby and London passed over the ford at Alport, where the volume of traffic led to a bridge being built in 1718. This was probably a packhorse route, there being an alternative route for wheeled traffic via Buxton and Brassington. The name Alport, found both here and at Alport Height, suggests 'old Portway', perhaps denoting a route that was already ancient when it was renamed in the early medieval period. This seems to be the only settlement which takes its name from the ancient road, and the OS map of 1896 shows it to have been a much busier place than it is today, with a flour mill, lime kilns and smelting works.

The pattern of roads in the Haddon Fields area was significantly altered in the late eighteenth century, as explained in detail by Cockerton. Interestingly, he states that this section of the Portway remains a 'public highway', though he adds that 'its use by motor cars ... is not, however, to be recommended'.[108]

Bridge over the River Lathkill at Alport.

The present condition of this stretch shows how rapidly a road can degenerate: beyond the barns there is no trace of a road surface. Two hundred yards to the west of the barns lies a tumulus in which Roman coins were found; another was sited at the junction with the Bakewell road, marked by two trees and just visible nowadays as a swelling in the ground next to the trig point.

The landscape here is remarkably tame compared to the region above Wirksworth: gentle slopes, few rocks, and large, productive fields. Parallel to the track to the east is the well-wooded range of hills above Haddon Hall. The predominant roadside tree is the ash, characteristic of these limestone uplands, which of course is reflected in the name of the next village to be reached. As was the case with previous Saxon settlements, the Portway here ignores the town of Bakewell and aims for a river crossing at Ashford-in-the-Water.

Guide stoop at the top of Crowhill Lane near Bakewell.

In the first of the field paths which bypass the town, between Haddon Fields and Crowhill Lane, it is possible to make out in the grass a raised bank running along the route. Clearly most of these small fields were enclosed in the eighteenth or nineteenth centuries, by which time the old track had become obsolete, but despite this the right of way was preserved. Consequently, this part of the route, with this footpath heading directly towards Ashford, is one of the best pieces of evidence for the Portway's existence. Furthermore, one part of this section was investigated by the Wirksworth Archaeological team who dug test pits to establish the sub-structure of the Roman road here, which was shown to be at least five metres wide.[109]

Crowhill Lane, which runs along the bottom of a wide, shallow valley, was not the original route into Ashford. Cockerton points out that the four-faced guide stoop[110] at the top of the lane is labelled Buxton, Tidswell *[sic]*, Winster and Bakewell. But today there are only three possible routes, which shows that the old road made directly for Ashford via a route which was largely erased when the turnpike was introduced, although the lower section still survives as John Bank Road. This joins the A6 almost opposite the lowest bridge, which may well be the site of the original ford, since the River Wye splits into several channels here.

Ashford-in-the-Water is a notably picturesque settlement, with three bridges over the Wye offering the watery views that always attract visitors. Only by walking this area can you appreciate how well chosen this crossing point was, since both east and west of Ashford the valley of the Wye has much steeper sides. The church of All Saints is probably sited near the original line of the Portway and has a lovely Romanesque tympanum showing the tree of life – presumably the ash, as in Norse mythology.

Tympanum of All Saints Church, Ashford.

123

WALKING: WINSTER TO ASHFORD-IN-THE-WATER (ABOUT 8 MILES)

From the crossroads on the B5056 above Winster, follow Islington Lane north to the junction with the Elton road. Cross this and then follow Dudwood Lane downhill until it rejoins the main road, where you follow the gated track uphill to Robin Hood's Stride.

The path is clearly marked, with a branch leading off to the right to the Hermitage and Cratcliff Rocks. After passing Robin Hood's Stride the main path crosses two meadows before joining the Elton to Alport road, where you turn right. This quiet lane provides a comfortable stroll of just over a mile to the river crossing. Ridge and furrow fields can be seen near Upper Greenfields Farm. Then the road corkscrews for the steep descent into the pretty village of Alport, where it crosses the river just above the millpond. It is notable that by crossing here, below the point where the River Lathkill meets the River Bradford, the route only needs to cross one valley and thus ford just one river, while keeping well away from the valley of the Wye to the east.

On the other side of the Youlgrave road take Dark Lane to climb steeply out of the valley and on to the plateau of Haddon Fields above. On reaching the straggling barns at the end of the road there are three public footpaths: that on the left leads to Conksbury Bridge while the one on the right is a bridleway to Haddon Hall. The line of the Portway runs straight ahead along the third path to the east of the wall and almost due north, until you join the road at a bend marked by a pair of trees. This road is shown on Burdett's map as the Bakewell to Newhaven turnpike, which crossed the Lathkill at Conksbury Bridge.

The route now runs downhill on the road for just under a mile before a footpath is marked on the left. Take this path, which runs first down to a stile, then across a narrow valley field and then up through several more fields. After crossing the busy road from Monyash to Bakewell the path becomes more tortuous as it wanders through a maze of small walled fields with numerous stiles, finally emerging onto the road just above Crowhill Lane. The old guide stoop can be found at the head of this lane, which gives a gentle descent down to the Wye Valley and the A6. This must be followed to the west for just under half a mile to Ashford-in-the-Water, but fortunately a pavement means there is no need to walk on the road.

Cross the river by the first bridge and then cross the A6020 into Church Street. The church is on the right, as is a decent pub selling Robinson's beer: The Bulls Head.

G. ASHFORD-IN-THE-WATER TO MAM TOR

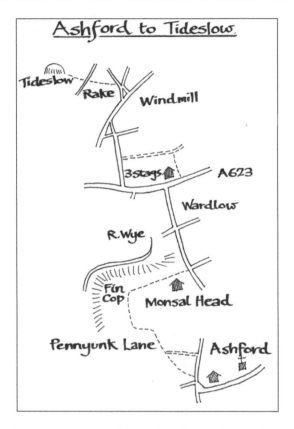

Today the direct route from Ashford to Monsal Head is on the busy B6465, but there is good evidence that the Portway followed the more circuitous route shown on the map as Pennyunk Lane. This curious name is probably Celtic in origin; Paul Brotherton[111] links it to Fin Cop and believes it may have meant something like 'headland of the youth'. 'Penn' means hilltop (Pennine may have the same root), and the lane passes just below the ten-acre site of Fin Cop, which overlooks the slopes of Monsal Dale. Fin Cop was the subject of an extensive excavation programme in 2009–2010 involving Longstone Local

History group.[112] Commonly described as an Iron Age hillfort, it was clearly a defensive site, protected partly by earth ramparts and partly by the steep drop into the Wye valley, and Bronze Age burials as well as Neolithic remains have been found within. It probably had different functions in different periods, and could certainly have sheltered travellers along the Portway.

Although parts of Pennyunk Lane would have been realigned when the land was enclosed and the stone walls built, it seems likely that this was the original route to Fin Cop, as well as being the main road north. The lane is now a pretty, tranquil walk, lined with low stone walls and the upland pastures of grazing cows. It is also well above the course of the main road, offering spectacular views to the north, east and south, and on the approach to Monsal Head the pointed summit of Wardlow Hay Cop (370m) to the north provides a useful marker. When the viewpoint at Monsal Head is reached it is clear that the route that has been followed (i.e. crossing the Wye at Ashford) is far easier than if the crossing had been made further upstream, where the river runs in a much deeper valley.

View of Fin Cop site from Monsal Head.

Monsal Head provides a good view of the Fin Cop site to the west, making full use of the defensive position provided by the bend in the river. The road north from here to Wardlow Mires is called Castlegate. The identity of the castle to which it led is unclear, but the route gives splendid views both east and west. The first two miles go steadily uphill, reaching a summit near Rolley Low on the left, which is the second burial mound on this stretch. On the other side of the road, under a hawthorn tree, is an old milestone with a benchmark cut into it, but unfortunately it is otherwise too worn to read.

The next stage runs downhill through the strung-out village of Wardlow. One feature of this area is the small walled fields on both sides of the road, which presumably reflect the complexity of land divisions at the time of enclosure. Tideslow becomes a more prominent landmark to the northwest as the path drops down. Wardlow Mires is surely one of the less attractive place names in Derbyshire, and the reality lives up to it.

The problem of the line of the Portway at Wardlow Mires is dealt with in some detail by R.W.P. Cockerton.[113] Briefly, he showed that the building of the Chesterfield turnpike not only obliterated this section, but also destroyed a sizeable barrow called Stoney Low which was close to the line of the road.

However, the lower part of Trot Lane, just north of the A623, is in alignment with the old route, and at the junction of Trot Lane with the track up to Stanley House, looking west, a very substantial holloway can be seen in the field leading directly towards Tideslow. This is one of those points where the existence of the ancient trackway appears conclusive, so clear is the evidence on the ground.

On the map it can be seen that this line continues both as field boundaries and as the parish boundary to the Little Hucklow road, after which it becomes lost in the very regular enclosure pattern of fields around Rising Sun Farm. The same line can be seen, looking back, from the top of Tideslow. This is the last significant landmark before

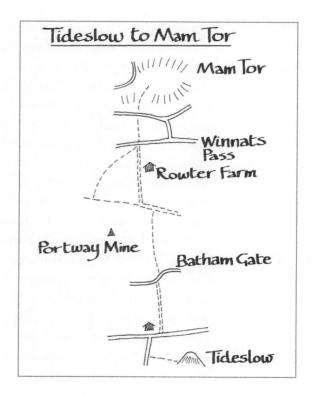

Mam Tor and it is clearly visible as one approaches ascending Tideslow Rake, a vivid scar from the days of lead mining. The whole summit of Tideslow has been extensively disturbed, at one time being used for a limekiln, which obscures the fact that it was the largest Neolithic round barrow in the county.[114] It appears to have been plundered first by lead miners and then dug by Victorian archaeologists, so that establishing its history is even more challenging than usual.

The route of the next stage of the Portway, from Tideslow to Mam Tor, has never been established, though the most obvious line runs north from Tideslow on a clear track. Although this is the most direct route, it has the drawback of not passing the site of the Portway Mine, shown on quite recent Ordnance Survey maps, which lies a few hundred yards to the west of this line. The simplest route, which is easier to navigate in poor weather, runs north to the east of Bushy Heath farm, then passes through a narrow belt of trees before crossing Batham Gate, the Roman road from Buxton to Brough. Looking south from here it can be seen that Tideslow was an effective landmark long before the nearby radio mast was erected. Cockerton[115] explained that the kink in the line of Batham Gate at this point shows that the Portway was in existence before the Romans arrived.

The route then crosses moorland, running downhill to meet a track below Rowter Farm, the only settlement on this section. There are good views along most parts of the route, especially to the east towards Hucklow, and constant reminders of the history of lead mining on the moor. Rakes and pits can be seen on both sides, and the OS map of 1896 gives the evocative names of some of the mines, such as Clear the Way, Starvehouse and Hazard. Before reaching the farm, Mam Tor – with its scar of landslip to the southeast face – becomes clearly visible, and soon the double horseshoe of ramparts can be made out. Crossing two roads, the track runs directly up to Mam Gap, from where there is a clear paved path to the summit.

Mam Tor from the south.

Given its prominent site and importance as the largest of Derbyshire's 'hillforts', as well as the excavation work that has been carried out here, it is surprising how little is known about Mam Tor. The name is thought to be Celtic, meaning breast, though perhaps the shape of the hill has changed over the millennia (it is also called the Shivering Mountain). There appears to have been either permanent or temporary settlement here for long periods, judging by the many hut bases that have been discovered.

Yet even if the climate was warmer, it is hard to imagine year-round settlement on a waterless site at over 500 metres. It has been suggested that the huts were for occupation in periods of conflict, or possibly by summer pastoralists, but they could equally have accommodated travellers. These hut sites, which may have been in use from 1100 BCE, as well as two Bronze Age barrows, seem to predate the ramparts, which belong to the Iron Age.

WALKING: ASHFORD-IN-THE-WATER TO MAM TOR (ABOUT 12 MILES)

Starting on Church Street in Ashford, walk past All Saints Church and turn right up Fennel Street. Either take the path signed to the left or continue to the top of the street where there is a track running northwest at Highfields. Both lead into Pennyunk Lane, which changes from a track to a field path before reaching the vicinity of Fin Cop. As it approaches the hamlet of Monsal Head the original line of the route is lost and the path emerges from the bushes directly above the dramatic railway viaduct.

The next three miles have to be walked on a fairly busy road, but the views offer some compensation for this. (The alternative is to drop down from Monsal Head to the track through Cressbrook Dale.) Castlegate runs nearly due north uphill for over a mile and a half to the crossroads with the road to Foolow. After this there is a pavement for the rest of the way through Wardlow to the junction with the busy A623.

The next stage cannot be walked on the line of the Portway, as no rights of way exist. The suggested route follows it quite closely, but clearly other options are possible. Turn right at the T-junction, go past the Three Stags pub, and take the footpath signed to the left. Follow the signs through the farmyard and then uphill towards Stanley House. Climb the stile here and join a narrow lane west. This leads to a junction with Trot Lane, where the line of the Portway as a holloway can be seen from the field gate opposite.

Take Trot Lane uphill to the junction with the B6049, turn right and go up to the hamlet of Windmill. From here a minor road runs uphill to the west, and just after leaving the houses behind traces of a mining rake can be seen, here known as High Rake. Take the track which forks off to the left along the rake and soon passes the excavations of High Rake Mine. The path crosses a road, and then it is necessary to keep close to the left-hand wall. The ground is heavily disturbed all the way up and all over the burial mound of Tideslow, from where there are excellent views back to Wardlow Mires.

The logical way from the top of Tideslow would be to go due north to join the clearly visible track leading to Mam Tor, but as there is no right of way it is necessary to go west to the road and then turn north past Bushey Heath Farm to link up with this route. Take the track to the east of the farm until it meets a metalled road. Follow the road north for a short distance until it bends to the east, then take the track north. This soon becomes a path on moorland, and eventually runs downhill to a junction of five ways. Go through the gate and then to the left, and after a hundred yards turn right towards Rowter Farm. This section runs over the hill and down to the B6061. Cross the road and follow the track over Windy Knoll to the base of Mam Tor.

H. EDALE TO THE WOODLANDS VALLEY

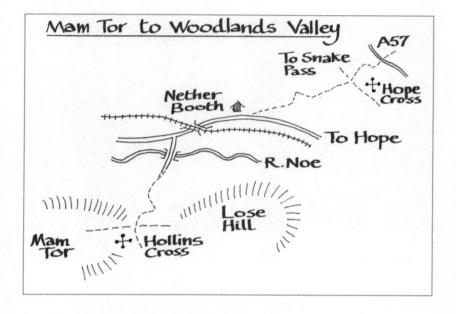

Beyond Mam Tor and Edale there is the most serious obstacle to north-south travel on the Portway: the high, bleak moors around Kinder Scout. The only realistic route for laden packhorses would be east along the Edale Valley and then up Edale End into the Woodlands Valley and over the Snake Pass to Glossop. This is partly the route the Romans took when they constructed a road from Navio, their fort at Brough, near Hope, northwest to another fort near modern-day Glossop. The route between Glossop and Hope is often called Doctor's Gate, named after a Dr John Talbot who was a vicar in Glossop in the sixteenth century. Given the high altitude and erosion that must have taken place over the centuries, it is difficult to date the existing tracks over the pass. Paving that was often considered to be Roman is thought by others to be medieval,[116] and it is likewise argued that Doctor's Gate was in fact a medieval road.

Path down from Hollins Cross northeast into Edale.

A fascinating insight into life in the Hope and Edale Valleys in the mid-nineteenth century is provided by A.J. Fletcher's study based on the 1851 census.[117] Although isolated geographically, the area was quite well connected with the major local centres: by turnpikes with Tideswell and Bakewell, and with coach and carrier services to Sheffield. A surprising third of the working population were factory workers or miners, while slightly fewer were farmers or agricultural workers. (These groups were quite fluid and some workers would have embodied both roles.) Clearly there was more industrial activity in the district then than there is today; for instance, the cotton mill in Edale employed more than 50 men from Castleton, who had to walk there via Hollins Cross every day: a formidable daily commute!

Overall, the study suggests a well-balanced community with a wide variety of employment and without a gentry class of landowners. Many of the upland farms were worked with just one or two labourers, and fewer than ten per cent of the workers were servants. Isolation meant that each village had to provide a good range of services; hence Edale had a baker, a butcher, a grocer, a general store and three inns. More remarkably, a wide variety of trades were found in the valleys: rope-makers, skinners, tanners, watchmakers, coopers, stay-makers, dressmakers, cloggers and tailors.

Above all, it is clear from Fletcher's research that, barren and remote though this area may seem today, its rugged paths and tracks were well used in the past. Speaking of five cloggers lodging at a farm in Hope Woodlands, he remarks:

> *This was perhaps the base from which they visited villages on both sides of the Pennines to set them up in clogs, or maybe they were itinerant workers temporarily resident on a main thoroughfare across the hills. Their presence, and the presence also in the valley when the census was taken of five hawkers, travellers in small wares and brushage, as well as a rag gatherer, reminds us of the huge wayfaring population, engaged in simple crafts and trades, of one kind or another, who tramped the roads of Victorian England.[118]*

A likely route from Mam Tor is the ridgeway down to Hollins Cross, which is now marked by a stone drum. This was a stage on the coffin path from Edale over to St Peter's Church at Hope. The actual cross has long since disappeared, but one can imagine that the coffin bearers were glad to rest at this point. From here a clear path drops down to Backtor Bridge over the River Noe, beyond which the road runs through Edale. This can be followed for half a mile through Nether Booth before a bridle way appears on the left. The first part of this is clearly an old holloway which runs behind Clough Farm and then gradually climbs to give good views out over lower Edale.

There is some place name evidence for this route: Jaggers Clough is a steep-sided valley crossed by the track higher up, and beyond this the line of the Roman road is reached. Logically, this is where Hope Cross would stand to indicate directions to Glossop, Sheffield, Hope and Edale. In fact, the cross is a few hundred yards back down the route to Hope, which may simply indicate a re-arrangement of the paths since it was erected in 1737 (possibly as a replacement for an earlier marker). Further up the north side of the Woodlands Valley, Alport Dale and Alport Bridge are to be found.

The Sheffield to Glossop turnpike, generally called the Snake Pass (because one of the principal investors was the Duke of Devonshire, whose symbol was a snake), was opened in 1821. It was the highest turnpike in England, reaching an altitude of 508 metres. Clearly the Duke and the other backers had no idea of the imminence of the railway age, which reduced the journey time from Sheffield to Manchester by more than half from 1845. As mentioned in Chapter 5, the turnpike trust never repaid its costs and was eventually wound up with large debts. Even today the pass is often closed in winter, and presumably in the era of travelling with horses its use would have been largely seasonal.

Hope Cross

WALKING: EDALE TO THE WOODLANDS VALLEY (ABOUT 4 MILES TO HOPE CROSS)

The paved path on the ridge between Mam Tor and Lose Hill is often busy, but below Hollins Cross there are usually few walkers. The track drops quite steeply in a northeasterly direction to Backtor Farm and then down to the bridge. Continue on the road in the same direction, going under the railway and through the hamlet of Nether Booth. Shortly after, a path forks off to the left and climbs towards the line of the Roman road on the ridge, an ascent broken by the crossing of Jaggers Clough.

From the col (i.e. the lowest point on the ridge) near Hope Cross the route of the Roman road can be followed northwest up the Snake Pass or southeast to Hope. Alternatively, by continuing northeast down to the A57 Manchester to Sheffield road and then up by Hagg Farm, the Ladybower Reservoir on the River Derwent can be reached.

9

Beyond the Portway

The Derbyshire Portway is remarkable in that it can be traced for over 60 miles, and for most of that distance it can be walked on public rights of way: mainly minor roads, tracks or footpaths. Clearly it would not have been the only long-distance route in medieval (or earlier) Derbyshire, however, and identifying some of the other routes is an interesting challenge.

It is perhaps surprising to find that none of the Roman roads can be walked today over any significant length, except as busy roads. The Street, for example, from Brassington to Buxton, has hardly any surviving rights of way, although part of the general route can be followed along the High Peak Trail. The same applies to most of Ryknild Street, which is mainly either main road or has disappeared without trace.

Dodd and Dodd[119] use place name evidence to suggest various 'saltways' running across Derbyshire from the salt sources (the 'wiches' such as Nantwich and Northwich) in the west. One of these runs from west to east via Leek, Brund, Hartington, Biggin and Pikehall, down Salters Lane into Matlock, and then on to Ashover where another Salters Lane can be found. Parts of this route are good walking terrain (over Bonsall Moor, for example) but most of it is along busy roads.

Nonetheless, I have identified three routes which offer rewarding walking and seem to have some historic validity. All of them should be walked using the Ordnance Survey 1:25,000 map for detailed directions. The following notes simply provide a general overview.

A. DOEHOLE LANE TO CROMFORD AND WIRKSWORTH (ABOUT 7 MILES)

Travellers would probably have used this route to go from Chesterfield or Ashover in the east to Wirksworth before a road (today's A6) was built through Matlock Bath.

The most easterly surviving guide stoop (illustrated on the cover of Howard Smith's book *Guide Stoops of Derbyshire*) is at the junction of Dethick Lane and the A615 Matlock to Alfreton road.[120] One of the towns named on the stone is Wirksworth, which seems surprising, given that there is no obvious route there today. But the stoop is dated 1710, at which time this would have been open moorland (see Chapter 5). Dethick Lane can be followed southeast, partly as a holloway, to the junction marked Cross Lanes on modern OS maps. The base of a cross, which presumably acted as a waymark, can be seen in the verge here. The road then continues to Dethick, an unusual hamlet consisting of three farmhouses and St John's Church (originally a chapel of ease for the Babington family of Dethick Manor).

From the church a path leads down past Swinepark Wood, over the brook and comes out on Lea Road just above the Jug and Glass Inn. Continue downhill and at the next junction a path cuts down through a meadow, crosses a road and continues down to the Lea Brook, which can normally be crossed on stepping stones. The path then runs uphill, first through a wood and then steeply over open pasture, with High Leas Farm on the right, to Hearthstone Lane. This lane is believed to be another ancient route, and can be followed south downhill past Castletop Farm and on to Cromford Bridge, but a more direct route is straight over the ridgeway. The path drops down sharply, first through a beech wood and then on pasture, after which it crosses a farm road and emerges near Cromford station.

From here the pavement continues to the bridge over the River Derwent, where the ruins of the chapel can be seen on the west bank (see Chapter 4) alongside the ornamental fishing pavilion built by Richard Arkwright. Continue past the mill, cross the A6, and then walk through the village of Cromford and up Cromford Hill. The original way into Wirksworth forked west off the modern B5036 at Dimons Dale. It then crossed Porter Lane and dropped down into the town following Old Lane.

B. BIRCHOVER TO CHESTERFIELD AREA (3–10 MILES)

The full length of this route is over 10 miles, but clearly it could be divided in half: the western end as far as Darley Bridge offers comfortable walking over about 3 miles.

On the B5056 opposite the track up to Robin Hood's Stride there is an informal lay-by. Near this a path climbs quite steeply eastwards, heading for the Druid's Inn at Birchover. But before approaching the village, take a right turn at the top of the slope and follow the path which runs along the contour line above Birchover Wood. When Birchover Lane is reached, turn briefly left and pick up Clough Lane to continue eastwards. This runs for over a mile to Oldfield Lane, and is shown on Burdett's map as running past two lead mines, Yate Stook and Mill Close. Near the junction sits the Enthoven Works, the recycled lead smelting factory, which gives a link to the days of working lead mines.

After crossing Darley Bridge, which has been here since at least 1500, a path to the right of The Square and Compass pub runs straight over the water meadows. This meets the appropriately named Old Road (which was the earlier highway between Bakewell and Matlock). Turn briefly right here and find a path running north, close to the showrooms of the DFS sofa company. This meets and crosses the A6 and continues up the hill to Two Dales.

The route then continues on Back Lane and Flash Lane, climbing towards the moors. An indication that this was a well-used route before the arrival of the turnpikes is provided by the guide stoop near Woodside Farm. Howard Smith[121] notes that this stone is unusual as it only shows one destination: Chesterfield (or Chasterfield as it is spelt here). Flash Lane continues on to East Moor, and from there minor roads provide a possible route to Holymoorside or Brampton. Flash was the site of a locally important livestock fair held bi-annually, mentioned by Mathew Gibbons in his diary (see Chapter 6).

C. WIRKSWORTH TO ASHOVER OR CHESTERFIELD (ABOUT 10 MILES TO ASHOVER)

This route between Wirksworth and northeast Derbyshire is steeper and more direct than the turnpike route which passes up Longway Bank from Whatstandwell Bridge, and it may well be medieval.

Leave Wirksworth via Wash Green, crossing the railway bridge and the infant River Ecclesbourne. When the road bends right a track can be found on the left; follow this up through the meadow and it emerges just below the Malt Shovel pub. Turn right here and follow the Belper road for a short distance to a track on the left. This leads into the parkland surrounding Wigley Grange. The path runs downhill into Park Wood and crosses a stream. In the next meadow, head east, aiming for the path which runs below Long Wood. Climb the slope beyond the wood but continue east until reaching a Peak and Northern Footpaths Society (PNFS) sign which marks the crossing of several paths (see picture in Chapter 7). Follow downhill for Whatstandwell, past a cottage, and the track emerges near the bridge across the Derwent.

Cross the Derwent and continue past the Family Tree café to the Cromford Canal. Here the old road pattern has been obscured by construction of both the railway and the canal, not to mention the excavations at Duke's Quarry. So the simplest route is to turn left along the canal towpath and walk a short distance to the pedestrian bridge. Cross this and fork left up to Leashaw Road. Cross this as well and continue on the path through the old quarry workings and the higher overgrown meadows to Wakebridge. Wakebridge Farm is on the site of Wakebridge Manor, and the track now runs uphill to the left of the farm. This is clearly an ancient route, being both a parish boundary and also the border between two wapentakes: Wirksworth and Morleyston and Litchurch.

The track becomes a field path before a barn and continues northeast to Shuckstone Fields, the crossing point of several paths. Here is the base of another wayside cross, similar to the one nearby at Cross Lanes (see route A above), and also a 'Holy Well' in a lower part of the field.[122] Continue along the same path, which emerges at the junction of Lea Moor Road and Shuckstone Lane. From here there are just over two miles of road walking.

Head northeast and take the first left, High Lane. At the end of this is the junction with the Matlock Road, and here is the guide stoop which marked the start of route A above. Cross the main road into Lickpenny Lane, which finishes by Scotland Nurseries (a popular garden centre). Cross the road here and continue for nearly a mile to the next major junction, where the traffic turns sharply left but the route goes straight on. The road now becomes a track and starts to drop down through Ravensnest into the upper Amber Valley. Cross several tracks and then drop steeply down again, partly on a causey [causeway], towards a narrow bridge over the River Amber and up into the village of Ashover on a stepped path. At the top of the steps the path joins the road conveniently close to the Old Poets' Corner pub.

Appendices

Appendix 1

DERBYSHIRE ROAD NAMES

The names of roads can be a useful tool for historians, yet they are often so familiar that we take them for granted. For example 'Steep Turnpike' in Matlock should alert researchers to the fact that this was part of the Chesterfield turnpike road in the late eighteenth century.

In order to analyse local naming, a sample of 95 road names was collected from the 1896 OS 25 inches to the mile map, sheet 34. This covers Bonsall, Matlock Bath, Cromford, Wirksworth, Lea and Whatstandwell. Surprisingly, despite their large scale, these maps do not name every road, but still include a fair sample nevertheless. The vast majority in the sample are called 'lanes', with 'streets' or 'roads' only occurring in built-up areas.

The most common type of name refers to the destination of the road:

Uppertown Lane
Alfreton Road
Riber Road

Or to some feature found on the road:
> *Blakelow Lane*
> *Wellhead Lane*
> *Pig Tor Lane*
> *Hearthstone Lane*
> *Bedehouse Lane*

Some refer to the condition or state of the road:
> *Causeway Lane*
> *Dark Lane* (quite common in Derbyshire and suggests a hollow way)
> *Long Lane*
> *Green Lane*
> *Hollowchurch Way*
> *Old Lane*

A few appear to be named after an individual:
> *Abel Lane*
> *Samuel Lane*
> *Rains's Lane*

Or may refer to the users of the road:
> *Salters Lane*
> *Sledgegate Lane*

And quite a large group are enigmatic:
> *Smuse Lane*
> *Lickpenny Lane*
> *Clatterway*
> *Fairy Lane*

Historians need to approach the subject with care, as confusion is easily caused. Shaw Lane at Lea, for example, may refer to a wood on a slope, but Shaw's Hill in Crich Carr was named after a Mr Shaw. Nonetheless, road names can provide valuable clues to the road patterns of the past, and details of the age and origin of a name can be found in Cameron.[123] For instance, he lists first references to some of the Bonsall names above as follows:

Abel Lane – 'John Abel 1670'

Clatterway – 'Lattered way 1620'

Wellhead Lane – 'Wellhead Pingle 1675'

Between Matlock and Chesterfield there is a group of lanes with 'stone' names:

Hearthstone Lane

Cuckoostone Lane

Wirestone Lane

Holestone Lane

Shuckstone Lane

The only surviving stone appears to be the Cuckoo Stone, now located on the Matlock Golf Club course, so presumably the others were broken up at some point. The names suggest that in the pre-enclosure period, when this area formed part of East Moor, these stones were significant features in the landscape.

Appendix 2

Appendix 3

JAMES CLEGG'S JOURNEYS: JANUARY – JUNE 1730

Date [monthly total]	Destination	Distance in miles	Total distance journeyed
Jan 1730 [69]	Martinside	1.5	3
	Whitehoughhead	1.5	3
	Cotebank	2	4
	Spire Hollins	2	4
	Whaley Bridge	3.5	7
	Slack Hall	1	2
	Ashford via Tideswell	14	28
	Ford and Malcoff	1	2
	Buxton – *snow had made the road bad*	7	14
	Ford	1	2
Feb [134]	Macclesfield – *I had dark travelling*	12	24
	Castleton	6	12
	Castleton – *much snow was fallen on the hills*	6	12
	Stanton in the Peak	19	38
	Manchester via Stockport	24	48
March [97]	Whaley Bridge	3.5	7
	Martinside	1.5	3
	Macclesfield	12	24
	Shireoaks	1	2

	Martinside – *the night being very dark I narrowly escaped a dangerous fall into a stone pitt which my mare jumped into*	1.5	3
	Shireoaks	1	2
	Castleton and Tideswell – *the day was rainy and cold*	12	12
	Castleton to Dronfield	16	16
	Dronfield to home	24	24
	Malcoff	1	2
	Castleton	6	12
April [163]	Buxton	7	14
	Edale End	5	10
	Whaley Bridge	3.5	7
	Castleton	6	12
	Buxton	7	14
	Ford	1	2
	Ashford	14	28
	Rochdale	27	27
	Rochdale to Manchester	11	11
	Manchester to home	20	20
	Shireoaks	1	2
	Whaley	3.5	7
	Wormhill and Martinside	2	4
	Lydgate	1	2
	Martinside	1.5	3
May [286]	Calow via Tideswell and Chesterfield	25	25
	Sutton Scarsdale Hall	2.5	5
	Calow to Derby via Offerton (Alfreton?)	25	25
	Derby to Calow	25	25

	Calow to Dronfield via Chesterfield and back to Chesterfield	10	10
	Chesterfield to Calow	1	1
	Calow to Chesterfield and back	2	2
	Calow to home via Middleton	35	35
	Slack Hall	1	2
	Macclesfield	12	24
	Buxton	7	14
	Manchester via Stockport	24	24
	Manchester to Rochdale and back	22	22
	Manchester to home	20	20
	Chinley Head	1	2
	Chinley Head	1	2
	Chinley Head, Buxton and Whaley Bridge	20	20
	Chinley Head	1	2
	Disley	6	12
	Buxton	7	14
June [193]	Ludworth	12	24
	Tideswell and Buxton	12	10
	Manchester via Stockport	24	24
	Manchester to home	20	20
	Macclesfield via Buxton	17	17
	Macclesfield to home	12	12
	Buxton	7	14
	Chesterfield via Dronfield	29	29
	Chesterfield to home via Tideswell	25	25
	Buxton	7	14
	Ford and Slack Hall	2	4

Appendix 4

MATHEW GIBBONS' TRAVELS 1761–2

Place (listed by frequency of visit)	Distance from Rowsley (miles)	Number of visits
Beeley	1.5	71
Bakewell	3.5	32
Darley	2	30
Edensor	3	11
Chesterfield	10	6
Matlock	4	6
Youlgrave	4	6
Baslow	5.5	4
Haddon	3	3
Ashford	5	3
Alport	2.5	3
Wingerworth	9	3
Winster	5	3
Birchover	4	2
Holymoorside	7.5	1
Longstone	7.5	1
Derby	24	1
Stanton	1.5	1

Appendix 5

THE PORTWAY ROUTE AND RELATED HISTORICAL SITES – SOUTHEAST TO NORTHWEST

Place	River crossing	Related historical sites	Place name evidence / Camps
Nottingham Trent Bridge		Highest point of river navigation/ hermitage	
Lenton Abbey	Leen	Cistercian abbey / Lenton Fair	
Wollaton		Arbour Hill	Defensive camp
Bramcote Hills		Hemlock Stone	
Church at Stapleford	Erewash	Cross	
Church at Sandiacre			Portway reference in charter
Dale Abbey		Hermitage / Arbour Hill	Defensive camp
Morley		Morley Mound / St Matthew's Church / Breadsall Priory	
Coxbench		St Anthony's Well / tumulus / Horsley Castle	
Holbrook		Roman pottery kilns	Portway road name
Makeney	Derwent	Holly Bush Inn	

Blackbrook		Quern production	
Alport Height		Guide stoop 1710	Defensive camp
Wirksworth		St Mary's Church / standing stone waymark	'Portway in Dalefield' reference
Griffe Grange		Harborough Rocks	Defensive camp / Portway reference in 1260 charter
Grangemill		Trace of Roman *aggar*	
Islington Lane		Guide stoop at Bonsall Lane junction	'Portaway Lane' 1764 enclosure
Dudwood Lane			Portaway Mine: Burdett 1761
Harthill Moor		Rock art / hermitage / stone circle	Defensive camp (Cratcliff Rocks)
Alport	Lathkill		
Haddon Fields		Tumulus / coin finds	Portway in manorial records
Ashford-in-the-Water	Wye	All Saints Church	
Monsal Head		Fin Cop	Defensive camp
Wardlow Mires		Tumulus (destroyed)	
Tideslow		Tumulus	Portway Mine
Mam Tor			Defensive camp

Edale Valley	Noe	Cross and chapel site on col	
Woodlands Valley		Roman road	Alport Bridge

Bibliography

Addison, Sir W. (1980) *The Old Roads of England*. London: Batsford

Alcock, L. (1973) *Arthur's Britain*. Harmondsworth: Penguin

Austen, J. (2003) *Mansfield Park*. Harmondsworth: Penguin

Bailey, S. (2008) *The Derbyshire Portway: Pilgrimage to the Past – a Walking Guide*. Cromford: Scarthin Books

Bennett, A. (2007) *The Old Wives' Tale*. Harmondsworth: Penguin

Bevan, B. (2004) *The Upper Derwent: 10,000 Years in a Peak District Valley*. Stroud: Tempus

Brassington, M. (1981) 'The Roman Roads of Derbyshire'. *Derbyshire Archaeological Journal* (DAJ) 101:88–92

Brighton, T. (2004) *The Discovery of the Peak District*. Chichester: Phillimore

Broadberry, S., Campbell, B. and Leeuwen, B. (2010) 'English Medieval Population: Reconciling Time Series and Cross Sectional Evidence'. Available at: https://warwick.ac.uk/fac/soc/economics/staff/sbroadberry/wp/medievalpopulation7.pdf

Brotherton, P. (2005) 'Celtic place names and archaeology in Derbyshire'. *Derbyshire Archaeological Journal* (DAJ) 125:100–137

Bunyan, J. (2008) *Pilgrim's Progress*. Harmondsworth: Penguin

Burdett, P. (1975 [1791]) *Map of Derbyshire*. Derby: Derbyshire Archaeological Society

Burke, T. (1942) *Travel in England*. London: Batsford

Byng, J. (1970) *The Torrington Diaries*. New York: Barnes and Noble

Cameron, K. (1959) *The Place Names of Derbyshire*. Cambridge: Cambridge University Press

Chaucer, G. (2005) *The Canterbury Tales*. Harmondsworth: Penguin

Cockerton, R.W.P. (1932–1936) *Derbyshire Countryside*; see Appendix 2

Coghill, N. (1951) *The Canterbury Tales: A New Translation*. Harmondsworth: Penguin

Currey, P.H. (1912) 'Notes on an ancient pack-horse bridge at Coxbench'. *Derbyshire Archaeological Journal* (DAJ) 34:1–4

Davies, D.H. (1811) *History of Derbyshire*. Belper: Mason

Davies, H. (2008) *Roman Roads in Britain*. Aylesbury: Shire

Defoe, D. (1928 [1724]) *A Tour of England and Wales*. London: Dent

Derbyshire County Record D4126/30

Dickens, C. (2000 [1836]) *The Pickwick Papers*. Harmondsworth: Penguin

Dodd, A. and Dodd, E. (1980 [1974]) *Peakland Roads and Trackways*. Ashbourne: Moorland

Doe, V. (ed.) (1981) *The Diary of James Clegg*. Derby: Derbyshire Record Society

Fiennes, C. (1888) *Through England on a Side Saddle in the Time of William and Mary*. London: Field and Tuer, The Leadenhall Press. Available at: http://www.visionofbritain.org.uk/travellers/Fiennes/15

Firth, J.B. (1908) *Highways and Byways in Derbyshire*. London: Macmillan

Fletcher, A.J. (1971) 'The Hope Valley in 1851'. *Derbyshire Archaeological Journal* (DAJ) 91:169–182

Gerhold, D. (2005) *Carriers and Coachmasters: Trade and Travel before the Turnpikes*. Bognor Regis: Phillimore

Guilbert, G., Garton D. and Walters, D. (2006) 'Prehistoric cup-and-ring art at the heart of Harthill Moor'. *Derbyshire Archaeological Journal* (DAJ) 126:12–30

Harrison, D. (2004) *The Bridges of Medieval England*. Oxford: Oxford University Press

Hey, D. (2004) *Packmen, Carriers and Packhorse Roads*. Ashbourne: Landmark

Hey, D. (2008) *Derbyshire: A History*. Lancaster: Carnegie

Hodges, R. (1991) *Wall-to-Wall History: The Story of Royston Grange*. London: Duckworth

Howe, D. (1984) *The Story of Holbrook*. Cromford: Scarthin

Hutton, R. (1996) *The Stations of the Sun*. Oxford: Oxford University Press

Lawrence, D.H. (1982) 'Love Among the Haystacks' in *Selected Short Stories*. Harmondsworth: Penguin

Lawrence, D.H. (1948 [1913]) *Sons and Lovers*. Harmondsworth: Penguin

Lawrence, D.H. (1995 [1915]) *The Rainbow*. Harmondsworth: Penguin

Macfarlane, R. (2012) *The Old Ways*. Harmondsworth: Penguin

Makepeace, G.A. (2004) 'Harborough Rocks: Early Iron Age settlement, near Brassington, Derbyshire. Second Report'. *Derbyshire Archaeological Journal* (DAJ) 124:64–68

Nottinghamshire Archives Ref: MP/RD/3L

Ogilby, J. (1939 [1675]) *Britannia. Volume 1: An Illustration of the Kingdom of England and Dominion of Wales by a Geographical and Historical Description of the Principal Roads Thereof*. Facsimile Reprint. Alexander Duckhams & Co

Orwell, G. (2001) *Down and Out in Paris and London*. Harmondsworth: Penguin

Palfreyman, A. (2001) 'Report on the excavation of a Romano-British aisled building at Little Hay Grange Farm, Ockbrook, Derbyshire 1994–97'. *Derbyshire Archaeological Journal* (DAJ) 121:70–161

Palfreyman, A. and Ebbins, S. (2007) 'A Romano-British quern manufacturing site at Blackbrook, Derbyshire'. *Derbyshire Archaeological Journal* (DAJ) 127:33–48

Pevsner, N. (1978) *Derbyshire*, Second Edition. Pevsner Architectural Guides: Buildings of England. New Haven, CT: Yale University Press.

Pilkington, J. (1789) *A View of the Present State of Derbyshire*, Volume II, p.218. Cited in Colvin, H.M. (1941) 'The internal history of Dale Abbey'. *Derbyshire Archaeological Journal* (DAJ) 62:31–57

Pryor, F. (2004) *Britain AD*. London: Harpur

Radley, J. and Plant, M. (1971) 'Tideslow: A Neolithic round barrow at Tideswell'. *Derbyshire Archaeological Journal* (DAJ) 91:20–30

Robb, G. (2014) *The Ancient Paths*. Basingstoke: Picador

Sanderson, G. (1835) *Map: Twenty Miles around Mansfield*. Nottingham: Nottinghamshire County Council

Shakespeare, W. (2005) *A Midsummer Night's Dream*. Harmondsworth: Penguin

Sharpe, N. (2002) *Crosses of the Peak District*. Ashbourne: Landmark

Shone, A. (2009) *Origins and History of Wirksworth: Lutudarum and the Peak District before the Norman Conquest*. Available at: https://duffieldcommunityorchard.files. wordpress.com/2014/03/wirksworth-history-lutudarum.pdf

Shone, A. and Smart, D. (2013) *The Derbyshire Portway: An archaeological assessment report*. Available from the Wirksworth Archaeological Society http://www. wirksworthromanproject.co.uk/

Shone, A. and Smart, D. (2017) *The Street: A Re-evaluation of the Roman Road from Wirksworth to Buxton*, p.6. Available from the Wirksworth Archaeological Society http://www.wirksworthromanproject.co.uk/

Smith, H. (2009 [1996]) *Guide Stoops of Derbyshire*. Ashbourne: Horizon

Spencer, C. (1993) *Walking the Derbyshire Portway: A Ramble Through History*. Hillsboro

Stone, R. (2005) *The River Trent*. Bognor Regis: Phillimore

Taylor, C. (1979) *Roads and Tracks of Britain*. London: Dent

Todd, A. (1994) *Two Years on a Derbyshire Farm: The Diary of Mathew Gibbons of Rowsley*. Bury: Allen and Todd

Turbutt, G. (2007) 'Unresolved mysteries of Derbyshire history'. *Derbyshire Archaeological Journal* (DAJ) 127:1–14

Twells, H. (1942) 'Mr Drewry and the Derby wagons'. *Derbyshire Archaeological Journal* (DAJ) 63:61–78

Twells, H. (1943) 'Derby's flying machines and earliest coaches'. *Derbyshire Archaeological Journal* (DAJ) 64:64–82

Ward, J. (1891) *Dale and its Abbey – Derbyshire*. Derby: Murray

Watkins, A. (1925) *The Old Straight Track*. London: Sphere

Webb, D. (2000) *Pilgrimage in Medieval England*. London: Hambledon Continuum

Whitelock, D. (1952) *The Beginnings of English Society*. Harmondsworth: Penguin

Willies, L. (2010) 'Matlock and the location of Domesday Mestesforde'. *Derbyshire Archaeological Journal* (DAJ) 103:176–188

Wiltshire, M. and Shone, A. (2016) *Wirksworth: A History*. Chesterfield: Bannister, pp.4–6

Wiltshire, M. and Woore, S. (2011) ' "Hays", possible early enclosures in Derbyshire'. *Derbyshire Archaeological Journal* (DAJ) 131:195–225

Wordsworth, D. (1986) *Home at Grasmere*. Harmondsworth: Penguin

Wroe, P. (1982) 'Roman Roads in the Peak District', *Derbyshire Archaeological Journal* (DAJ) 102:49–73

Wroe, P. (2000) *A Roman Road between the Roman Fort Navio at Brough-on-Noe and Melandra Castle, Glossop*. Publisher unknown.

Endnotes

1   Gerhold, D. (2005) *Carriers and Coachmasters: Trade and Travel before the Turnpikes*. Bognor Regis: Phillimore

2   Burdett, P. (1975 [1791]) *Map of Derbyshire*. Derby: Derbyshire Archaeological Society

3   Sanderson, G. (1835) *Map: Twenty Miles around Mansfield*. Nottingham: Nottinghamshire County Council

4   Shone, A. and Smart, D. (2017) *The Street: A Re-evaluation of the Roman Road from Wirksworth to Buxton*, p.6. Available from the Wirksworth Archaeological Society http://www.wirksworthromanproject.co.uk/

5   Hodges, R. (1991) *Wall to Wall History: The Story of Royston Grange*. London: Duckworth, p.65

6   In line with most historical work, this book uses the modern convention of BCE to denote 'before the common era (i.e. BC) and CE to denote 'common era' (i.e. AD)

7   Taylor, C. (1979) *Roads and Tracks of Britain*. London: Dent, p.8

8   Bevan, B. (2004) *The Upper Derwent: 10,000 Years in a Peak District Valley*. Stroud: Tempus

9   Hey, D. (2008) *Derbyshire: A History*. Lancaster: Carnegie

10 Stone, R. (2005) *The River Trent*. Bognor Regis: Phillimore

11 Dodd, A. and Dodd, E. (1980 [1974]) *Peakland Roads and Tracks*. Ashbourne: Moorland, p.20

12 Brassington, M. (1981) 'The Roman Roads of Derbyshire'. *Derbyshire Archaeological Journal* (DAJ) 101:88–92

13 Wroe, P. (1982) 'Roman Roads in the Peak District', *Derbyshire Archaeological Journal* (DAJ) 102:49–73

14 Shone, A. and Smart, D. (2017) *The Street: A Re-evaluation of the Roman Road from Wirksworth to Buxton*, p.6. Available from the Wirksworth Archaeological Society http://www.wirksworthromanproject.co.uk/

15 Alcock, L. (1973) *Arthur's Britain*. Harmondsworth: Penguin, p.317

16   Pryor, F. (2004) *Britain AD*. London: Harpur, p.213

17   Webb, D. (2000) *Pilgrimage in Medieval England*. London: Hambledon Continuum

18   Whitelock, D. (1952) *The Beginnings of English Society*. Harmondsworth: Penguin

19   Broadberry, S., Campbell, B. and Leeuwen, B. (2010) 'English Medieval Population: Reconciling Time Series and Cross Sectional Evidence'. https://warwick.ac.uk/fac/soc/economics/staff/sbroadberry/wp/medievalpopulation7.pdf

20   Willies, L. (2010) 'Matlock and the location of Domesday Mestesforde'. *Derbyshire Archaeological Journal* (DAJ) 103:176–188

21   Harrison, D. (2004) *The Bridges of Medieval England*. Oxford: Oxford University Press

22   Coghill, N. (1951) *The Canterbury Tales: A New Translation*. Harmondsworth: Penguin, p.25

23   Burke, T. (1942) *Travel in England*. London: Batsford

24   Gerhold, D. (2008) *Carriers and Coachmasters: Trade and Travel before the Turnpikes*. Bognor Regis: Phillimore

25   Hey, D. (2004) *Packmen, Carriers and Packhorse Roads*. Ashbourne: Landmark, pp.68–75

26   Shakespeare, W. (2005) *A Midsummer Night's Dream*. Harmondsworth: Penguin, Act V, Scene II

27   Wiltshire, M. and Woore, S. (2011) ' "Hays", possible early enclosures in Derbyshire'. *Derbyshire Archaeological Journal* (DAJ) 131:195–225

28   Smith, H. (2009 [1996]) *Guide Stoops of Derbyshire*. Ashbourne: Horizon, p.79

29   Derbyshire County Record D4126/30

30   Dodd, A. and Dodd, E. (1980 [1974]) *Peakland Roads and Trackways*. Ashbourne: Moorland, p.132

31   Twells, H. (1942) 'Mr Drewry and the Derby wagons'. *Derbyshire Archaeological Journal* (DAJ) 63:61–78

32   Twells, H. (1943) 'Derby's flying machines and earliest coaches'. *Derbyshire Archaeological Journal* (DAJ) 64:64–82

33   Dickens, C. (2000 [1836]) *The Pickwick Papers*. Harmondsworth: Penguin

34   Wordsworth, D. (1986) *Home at Grasmere*. Harmondsworth: Penguin

35   Hey, D. 2004, *Packmen, Carriers and Packhorse Roads*. Ashbourne: Landmark

36   Lawrence, D.H. (1982) *The White Peacock*. Harmondsworth: Penguin

37   Information supplied by Geoff Lester of Winster

38   Orwell, G. (2001) *Down and Out in Paris and London.* Harmondsworth: Penguin

39   Lawrence, D.H. (1982) 'Love among the Haystacks' in *Selected Short Stories.* Harmondsworth: Penguin, p.46

40   Wordsworth, D. (1986) *Home at Grasmere.* Harmondsworth: Penguin

41   Dodd, A. and Dodd, E. (1980 [1974]) *Peakland Roads and Trackways.* Ashbourne: Moorland, p.129

42   Ogilby, J. (1939 [1675]) *Britannia. Volume 1: An Illustration of the Kingdom of England and Dominion of Wales by a Geographical and Historical Description of the Principal Roads Thereof.* Facsimile Reprint. Alexander Duckhams & Co. Available at: https://www.fulltable.com/vts/m/map/ogilby/mna.htm

43   Smith, H. (2009 [1996]) *Guide Stoops of Derbyshire.* Horizon: Ashbourne

44   Fiennes, C. (1888) *Through England on a Side Saddle in the Time of William and Mary.* London: Field and Tuer. The Leadenhall Press. Available at: http://www.visionofbritain.org.uk/travellers/Fiennes/15

45   Defoe, D. (1928 [1724]) *A Tour of England and Wales, volume 2.* London: Dent, p.158

46   Byng, J. (1970) *The Torrington Diaries.* New York: Barnes and Noble

47   Doe, V. (ed.) (1981) *The Diary of James Clegg.* Derby: Derbyshire Record Society

48   Todd, A. (1994) *Two Years on a Derbyshire Farm: The Diary of Mathew Gibbons of Rowsley.* Bury: Allen and Todd

49   Doe, V. (ed.) (1981) *The Diary of James Clegg.* Derby: Derbyshire Record Society

50   Brighton, T. (2004) *The Discovery of the Peak District.* Chichester: Phillimore

51   Jane Austen never visited Derbyshire, so clearly the principal attractions of the county were well known further afield.

52   Defoe, D. (1928 [1724]) *A Tour of England and Wales.* London: Dent, p.160

53   Cited in: Davies, D.H. (1811) *History of Derbyshire.* Belper: Mason, pp.468–9

54   Brighton, T. (2004) *The Discovery of the Peak District.* Chichester: Phillimore

55   Lawrence, D.H. (1995 [1915]) *The Rainbow.* Harmondsworth: Penguin, p.22

56   Bennett, A. (1986 [1908]) *The Old Wives' Tale.* Harmondsworth: Penguin

57   Lawrence, D.H. (1948 [1913]) *Sons and Lovers.* Harmondsworth: Penguin, pp.207–8

58   Today called The Peak and Northern Footpaths Society. See: http://www.peakandnorthern.org.uk/index.htm

59   Now called The Derbyshire Archaeological Society. See: https://www.derbyshireas.org.uk/

60   Brighton, T. (2004) *The Discovery of the Peak District*. Chichester: Phillimore, p.201

61   See: http://www.nottshistory.org.uk/articles/mellorsarticles/sneinton2.htm

62   See: http://www.nottshistory.org.uk/articles/mellorsarticles/sneinton1.htm

63   Although extensively remodelled in the early twentieth century

64   See: http://www.lentontimes.co.uk/images/gallery/castle_boulevard/castle_boule_listener_39.htm

65   See: http://www.lentontimes.co.uk/images/gallery/priory_street/priory_st_listener_49.htm

66   Nottinghamshire Archives Ref: MP/RD/3L

67   See: http://www.nottshistory.org.uk/articles/tts/tts1936/lenton/lenton9.htm

68   Hutton, R. (1996) *The Stations of the Sun*. Oxford: Oxford University Press

69   Lawrence, D.H. (1948 [1913]) *Sons and Lovers*. Harmondsworth: Penguin, p.204

70   Pevsner, N. (1978) *Derbyshire*, Second Edition. Pevsner Architectural Guides: Buildings of England. New Haven, CT: Yale University Press, p.312

71   Cockerton, R.W.P. (1935a); see Appendix 2 for a list of all the articles by R.W.P. Cockerton relating to the Derbyshire Portway

72   *Ibid.*

73   Cockerton, R.W.P. (1935b)

74   Palfreyman, A. (2001) 'Report on the excavation of a Romano-British aisled building at Little Hay Grange Farm, Ockbrook, Derbyshire 1994–97'. *Derbyshire Archaeological Journal* (DAJ) 121:70–161

75   Ward, J. (1891) *Dale and its Abbey – Derbyshire*. Derby: Murray

76   *Ibid.*

77   Pilkington, J. (1789) *A View of the Present State of Derbyshire*, Volume II, p.218. Cited in Colvin, H.M. (1941) 'The internal history of Dale Abbey'. *Derbyshire Archaeological Journal* (DAJ) **62**:31–57

78   Pevsner, N. (1978) *Derbyshire*, Second Edition. Pevsner Architectural Guides: Buildings of England. New Haven, CT: Yale University Press, p.163

79   Ward, J. (1891) *Dale and its Abbey – Derbyshire*. Derby: Murray

80   Pevsner, N. (1978) *Derbyshire*, Second Edition. Pevsner Architectural Guides: Buildings of England. New Haven, CT: Yale University Press, p.283

81   Currey, P.H. (1912) 'Notes on an ancient pack-horse bridge at Coxbench'. *Derbyshire Archaeological Journal* (DAJ) **34**:1–4

82   Cockerton, R.W.P. (1936a)

83   Davies, D. (1811) *History of Derbyshire*. Belper: Mason

84   Howe, D. (1984) *The Story of Holbrook*. Cromford: Scarthin

85   *Ibid.*

86   *Ibid.*

87   Cameron, K. (1959) *The Place Names of Derbyshire*. Cambridge: Cambridge University Press

88   Palfreyman, A. and Ebbins, S. (2007) 'A Romano-British quern manufacturing site at Blackbrook, Derbyshire'. *Derbyshire Archaeological Journal* (DAJ) 127:33–48

89   Spencer, C. (1993) *Walking the Derbyshire Portway: A Ramble Through History*. Hillsboro

90   Smith, H. (2009 [1996]) *Guide Stoops of Derbyshire*. Ashbourne: Horizon

91   Wiltshire, M. and Shone, A. (2016) *Wirksworth: A History*. Chesterfield: Bannister, pp.4–6

92   Turbutt, G. (2007) 'Unresolved mysteries of Derbyshire history'. *Derbyshire Archaeological Journal* (DAJ) 127:1–14

93   'Bole' indicates a wind-driven ore smelter

94   Cockerton, R.W.P. (1936b)

95   Shone, A. (2009) *Origins and History of Wirksworth: Lutudarum and the Peak District before the Norman Conquest*. Available at: https://duffieldcommunityorchard.files.wordpress.com/2014/03/wirksworth-history-lutudarum.pdf

96   Shone, A. and Smart, D. (2017) *The Street: A Re-evaluation of the Roman Road from Wirksworth to Buxton*. Available from the Wirksworth Archaeological Society http://www.wirksworthromanproject.co.uk/

97   Defoe, D. (1928 [1724]) *A Tour of England and Wales*. London: Dent, p.162

98   Makepeace, G.A. (2004) 'Harborough Rocks: Early Iron Age settlement, near Brassington, Derbyshire. Second Report'. *Derbyshire Archaeological Journal* (DAJ) 124:64–68

99   Shone, A. and Smart, D. (2013) *The Derbyshire Portway: An archaeological assessment report*. Available from the Wirksworth Archaeological Society http://www.wirksworthromanproject.co.uk/

100   Cockerton, R.W.P. (1934c)

101   Smith, H. (2009 [1986]) *Guide Stoops of Derbyshire*. Ashbourne: Horizon, pp.36–37

102   *Ibid.*

103   It is also named on Burdett's map

104   Guilbert, G., Garton D. and Walters, D. (2006) 'Prehistoric cup-and-ring art at the heart of Harthill Moor' *Derbyshire Archaeological Journal* (DAJ) 126:12–30

105   Cockerton, R.W.P. (1934b)

106 *Ibid.*

107 Cockerton, R.W.P. (1934a)

108 Cockerton, R.W.P. (1934a, p.21); today it is a restricted byway

109 Shone, A. and Smart, D. (2013) *The Derbyshire Portway: An archaeological assessment report.* Available from the Wirksworth Archaeological Society http://www.wirksworthromanproject.co.uk/

110 Cockerton R.W.P. (1932b); the guide stoop was originally on the other side of the road

111 Brotherton, P. (2005) 'Celtic place names and archaeology in Derbyshire'. *Derbyshire Archaeological Journal* (DAJ) 125:100–137

112 See: https://www.archaeologicalresearchservices.com/projects/fin-cop-hillfort/

113 Cockerton, R.W.P. (1932d)

114 Radley, J. and Plant, M. (1971) 'Tideslow: A Neolithic round barrow at Tideswell'. *Derbyshire Archaeological Journal* (DAJ) 91:20–30

115 Cockerton, R.W.P. (1933a)

116 Wroe, P. (2000) *A Roman Road between the Roman Fort Navio at Brough-on-Noe and Melandra Castle, Glossop.* Publisher unknown.

117 Fletcher, A.J. (1971) 'The Hope Valley in 1851'. *Derbyshire Archaeological Journal* (DAJ) 91:169–182

118 *Ibid.,* p.179

119 Dodd, A. and Dodd, E. (1980 [1974]) *Peakland Roads and Trackways.* Ashbourne: Moorland, pp.119–125

120 The stone is not in its original position, but the directions marked on it still apply

121 Smith, H. (2009 [1996]) *Guide Stoops of Derbyshire.* Ashbourne: Horizon, p.77

122 For more detail on this area see: http://www.crichparish.co.uk/webpages/shuckstone.html

123 Cameron, K. (1959) *The Place Names of Derbyshire.* Cambridge: Cambridge University Press

124 Gerhold, D. (2005) *Carriers and Coachmasters: Trade and Travel before the Turnpikes.* Bognor Regis: Phillimore

125 Burdett, P. (1975 [1791]) *Map of Derbyshire.* Derby: Derbyshire Archaeological Society

126 Sanderson, G. (1835) *Map: Twenty Miles around Mansfield.* Nottingham: Nottinghamshire County Council

127 Shone, A. and Smart, D. (2017) *The Street: A Re-evaluation of the Roman Road from Wirksworth to Buxton,* p.6. Available from the Wirksworth Archaeological Society http://www.wirksworthromanproject.co.uk/

Follow my blog on the history of Derbyshire's roads at:

www.oldroadsofderbyshire.com